Ruby Performance Optimization

Why Ruby Is Slow, and How to Fix It

Alexander Dymo

The Pragmatic Bookshelf

Dallas, Texas • Raleigh, North Carolina

Many of the designations used by manufacturers and sellers to distinguish their products are claimed as trademarks. Where those designations appear in this book, and The Pragmatic Programmers, LLC was aware of a trademark claim, the designations have been printed in initial capital letters or in all capitals. The Pragmatic Starter Kit, The Pragmatic Programmer, Pragmatic Programming, Pragmatic Bookshelf, PragProg and the linking *g* device are trademarks of The Pragmatic Programmers, LLC.

Every precaution was taken in the preparation of this book. However, the publisher assumes no responsibility for errors or omissions, or for damages that may result from the use of information (including program listings) contained herein.

Our Pragmatic courses, workshops, and other products can help you and your team create better software and have more fun. For more information, as well as the latest Pragmatic titles, please visit us at *https://pragprog.com*.

The team that produced this book includes:

Michael Swaine (editor)
Potomac Indexing, LLC (index)
Liz Welch (copyedit)
Dave Thomas (layout)
Janet Furlow (producer)
Ellie Callahan (support)

For international rights, please contact *rights@pragprog.com*.

Printed in the United States of America.
ISBN-13: 978-1-68050-069-1
Printed on acid-free paper.
Book version: P1.0—December 2015

Early praise for *Ruby Performance Optimization*

This book is a must-have for anyone bringing performance-sensitive Ruby programs to production. It will teach you how to efficiently hunt down and correct the bottlenecks that make users sad and prevent teams from spending time building new functionality.

➤ **Matt Margolis**
   Director of application development, Getty Images

A fantastic book. Probably the best tech book I have read in the last few years. It brings together information I can't just find in 30 minutes of web searches. This book has taught me to be a better developer and to start filling a hole in my skill set.

➤ **Charley Stran**
   Web developer, TheBlaze | Mercury Radio Arts

Ruby Performance Optimization has changed the way I develop. I now think about simple performance tweaks before I commit code. It is a book I keep close for reference when solving tough performance issues.

➤ **Jeff Holland**
   Senior software engineer, Ackmann & Dickenson

For programmers who aren't familiar with what is going on "under the covers," I think this book will open their eyes to new levels of understanding their code.

➤ **Kim Shrier**
   Principal, Westryn Internet Services, Shrier and Deihl

To my wife Helen and my daughter Sophia.

Contents

Preface

While I was writing this book, Ruby turned 21. During those two decades the Ruby core team has steadily evolved the language and stabilized standard libraries, the Ruby community has developed a whole ecosystem of advanced tools, and Rubygems has pretty much become a source of solutions for all of a Ruby developer's needs. But one nagging little concern has always remained: performance.

The Need for Speed

It's a widely shared belief that Ruby is slooow. Ruby, the common wisdom says, is a lovely language that saves you time while you're developing your application but drags its feet when you execute it. How much truth is there to that belief?

Well, good old Ruby 1.8, released in 2003, was indeed slow. But since then Ruby developers have radically improved the language's performance. Ruby 1.9 added a virtual machine that executes the code faster. Ruby 2.0 has copy-on-write friendly memory management that makes large web application deployments faster. And finally, thanks to the outstanding work of Koichi Sasada, Ruby got a generational garbage collector in version 2.1 and an incremental garbage collector in 2.2. That work continues and better performance is now one of the primary goals of the new releases.

So how slow is Ruby now? Not so slow: it's now on par with other dynamic languages. And how slow are Ruby applications now? Ah, that depends. A lot of legacy code exists that still runs Ruby 1.8 or 1.9 with little to no possibility to upgrade. You can assume that it's slow. But more importantly, there is a whole lot of Ruby code that was written without performance in mind. And that code will stay slow no matter which Ruby version you run.

I have been developing Ruby and Rails applications since 2006. I have seen slow Ruby code everywhere. And now in 2015 I still have to spend as much time optimizing my code as I did back in 2006—even when I use the latest and fastest Ruby.

You might very well be wondering why I bother to optimize code when there are other, better-known ways to make an application run faster—namely caching and scaling. Both techniques are well known and understood. You'll have no trouble finding plenty of advice on caching strategies, as well as many scaling recipes, and some very good tools are available for caching and scaling.

And you're right, caching and scaling do help with performance. I used to do both. But one day my cache invalidation code became too complex. Another day I found myself spending too much money on servers and Heroku dynos. Then there was the time when my long-running asynchronous processes ran around the clock and still struggled to serve incoming jobs in time. That was the point at which I started looking at code optimization. I wanted to make my programs run faster and use fewer resources. It turned out code optimization is the only way to do that more cheaply and without overcomplicating the application architecture.

To my surprise I found no good single source of information on Ruby code optimization. Resources you can find online are either technical descriptions of Ruby internals or advice on micro-optimizations like the recommendation to use instance variables instead of method calls. But knowledge of the internals is not useful without an understanding of the big picture. Micro-optimizations sometimes work, but most times they're simply too low-level to be effective.

I learned code optimization myself the hard way and wrote this book so you don't have to tread that hard path. In this book you'll learn why Ruby code becomes slow, how to make it faster, and what tools to use to do it. I hope you'll also grow to enjoy code optimization as much as I do. It is a very rewarding process: you dig the details, you build the big picture in your mind, make a change, and measure a difference. And you instantly know how big/important your change is. This is the second shortest reward cycle I know after writing "Hello World" in a new language.

How to Read This Book

This book starts by demonstrating simple Ruby and Rails performance optimization tips and tricks. Then you'll see how to use profiling tools to optimize when simple changes no longer work. You'll learn how to measure the optimization effect, and how to write tests to ensure the performance does not degrade after the optimization. You'll also learn to tune up both the deployment infrastructure and the Ruby interpreter itself for optimal performance.

The complexity of material gradually increases as the book goes on. So, if you are new to performance optimization, your best bet would be to read it from start to finish. Otherwise, feel free to skip chapters, or even read in your own order.

At the website for this book[1] you'll find the full source code for all the example programs used in this book; an errata page that lists mistakes in the current edition; and a discussion forum, where you can talk to the author and other people interested in Ruby performance optimization.

Acknowledgments

This book took more than a year for me to complete, and I'd like to acknowledge a few people who helped me make it happen.

First, my editor Michael Swaine and the folks at the Pragmatic Bookshelf. I've always admired your work. Thanks for giving me the chance to write my first book with you.

Gleb Arshinov, who introduced me to the world of performance optimization. Thanks, Gleb.

My tech reviewers Sam Ruby, Alessandro Bahgat, Charley Stran, Kevin Gisi, Jeff Holland, Matthew Margolis, and Kim Shrier. Your feedback helped me to reorganize my thoughts to make this book much better. Thanks.

Special thanks go to my family for their continued support of all my endeavors, no matter how crazy, lengthy, or surprising they are.

Now let's start optimizing!

Alexander Dymo
alex@alexdymo.com
Chicago, November 2015

---

1. https://pragprog.com/book/adrpo

## CHAPTER 1

What Makes Ruby Code Fast

It's time to optimize.

This is what I think when my Heroku dyno restarts after logging an "R14 - Memory quota exceeded" message. Or when New Relic sends me another bunch of Apdex score alerts. Or when simple pages take forever to load and the customer complains that my application is too slow. I'm sure you've had your own "time to optimize" moments. And every time these moments occur, we both ask exactly the same question: "What can I do to make the code faster?"

In my career as a Ruby programmer I have learned that the immediate answer to this question is often "I don't know." I'll bet that's your experience, too. After all, you thought you were writing efficient code. What we typically do then is to skip optimization altogether and resort to caching and scaling. Why? Because we don't immediately see how to improve the code. Because conventional wisdom says optimization is hard. And because caching and scaling are familiar to seasoned Ruby developers. In most cases you only need to configure some external tool and make minimal changes to the code, and voilà! Your code is faster.

But there is a limit to what caching and scaling can do for you. One day my company discovered that Hirefire, the automated scaling solution for Heroku, scaled up the number of Heroku web dynos to 36 just to serve a meager five requests per minute. We would have to pay $3,108 per month for that. And our usual bill before was $228 for two web dynos and one worker. Whoa, why did we have to pay almost fifteen times more? It turned out there were two reasons for that. First, web traffic increased. Second, our recent changes in the code made the application three times slower. And our traffic kept increasing, which meant that we'd have to pay even more. Obviously, we needed a different approach. This was a case where we hit a limit to scaling and had to optimize.

It is also easy to hit a limit with caching. You can tell that you need to stop caching when your cache key gets more and more granular.

Let me show you what I mean with a code snippet from a Rails application of mine:

```ruby
cache_key = [@org.id, @user.id,
  current_project, current_sprint, current_date,
  @user_filter, @status_filter,
  @priority_filter, @severity_filter, @level_filter]

cache(cache_key.join("_")) do
  render partial: 'list'
end
```

Here my cache key consists of ten parts. You can probably guess that the likelihood of hitting such a granular cache is very low. This is exactly what happened in reality. At some point my application started to spend more resources (either memory for Memcached or disk space) for caching than for rendering. Here's a case where further caching would not increase performance and I again had to optimize.

So have I convinced you of the need to optimize? Then let's learn how.

Here's when most sources on performance optimization start talking about execution time, profilers, and measurements. The hard stuff. We'll do our own share of profiling and measuring, but let's first step back and think about what exactly we need to optimize. Once we understand what makes Ruby slow, optimization stops being a search for a needle in a haystack with the profiler. Instead it can become almost a pleasing task where you attack a specific problem and get a significant performance improvement as the reward.

What Makes Ruby Code Slow

To learn what makes Ruby code fast, we must understand what makes Ruby code slow.

If you've done any performance optimization in the past, you probably think you know what makes code slow. You may think that even if you haven't done performance optimization. Let me see if I can guess what you think.

Your first guess is algorithmic complexity of the code: extra nested loops, computations, that sort of stuff. And what would you do to fix the algorithmic complexity? Well, you would profile the code, locate the slow section, identify the reason for the slowness, and rewrite the code to avoid the bottleneck. Rinse and repeat until fast.

Sounds like a good plan, right? However, it doesn't always work for Ruby code. Algorithmic complexity can be a major cause for performance problems. But Ruby has another cause that developers often overlook.

Let me show you what I'm talking about. Let's consider a simple example that takes a two-dimensional array of strings and formats it as a CSV.

Let's jump right in. Key in or download this simple program.

chp1/example_unoptimized.rb
```ruby
require "benchmark"

num_rows = 100000
num_cols = 10
data = Array.new(num_rows) { Array.new(num_cols) { "x"*1000 } }

time = Benchmark.realtime do
  csv = data.map { |row| row.join(",") }.join("\n")
end

puts time.round(2)
```

We'll run the program and see how it performs. But before that we need to set up the execution environment. There are five major Ruby versions in use today: 1.8.7, 1.9.3, 2.0, 2.1, and 2.2. These versions have very different performance characteristics. Ruby 1.8 is the oldest and the slowest of them, with a different interpreter architecture and implementation. Ruby 1.9.3 and 2.0 are the current mainstream releases with similar performance. Ruby 2.1 and 2.2 are the only versions that were developed with performance in mind, at least if we believe their release notes, and thus should be the fastest.

It's hard to target old software platforms, so I'll make a necessary simplification in this book. I will neither write examples nor measure performance for Ruby 1.8. I do this because Ruby 1.8 is not only internally different, it's also source-incompatible, making my task extremely complicated. However, even if you have a legacy system running Ruby 1.8 with no chance to upgrade, you can still use the performance optimization advice from this book. Everything I describe in the book applies to 1.8. In fact, you might even get more improvement. The old interpreter is so inefficient that any little change can make a big difference. In addition to that I will give 1.8-specific advice where appropriate.

The easiest way to run several Rubys without messing up your system is to use rbenv or rvm. I'll use the former in this book. Get rbenv from https://github.com/sstephenson/rbenv. Follow the installation instructions from README.md. Once you install it, download the latest releases of Ruby versions that you're interested in. This is what I did; you may want to get more recent versions:

```
$ rbenv install -l
  ...
  1.9.3-p551
  2.0.0-p598
  2.1.5
  2.2.0
  ...
$ rbenv install -k 1.9.3-p551
$ rbenv install -k 2.0.0-p598
$ rbenv install -k 2.1.5
$ rbenv install -k 2.2.0
```

Note how I install Ruby interpreters with the k option. This keeps sources in rbenv's directory after compilation. In due time we'll talk about the internal Ruby architecture and implementation, and you might want to have a peek at the source code. For now, just save it for the future.

To run your code under a specific Ruby version, use this:

```
$ rbenv versions
* system (set by /home/user/.rbenv/version)
  1.9.3-p551
  2.0.0-p598
  2.1.5
  2.2.0
$ rbenv shell 1.9.3-p551
$ ruby chp1/example_unoptimized.rb
```

To get a rough idea of how things perform, you can run examples just one time. But you shouldn't make comparisons or draw any conclusions based on only one measurement. To do that, you need to obtain statistically correct measurements. This involves running examples multiple times, statistically post-processing the measurement results, eliminating external factors like power management on most modern computers, and more. In short, it's hard to obtain truly meaningful measurement. We will talk about measurements later in Chapter 7, *Measure*, on page 103. But for our present purposes, it is fine if you run an example several times until you see the repeating pattern in the numbers. I'll do my measurements the right way, skipping any details of the statistical analysis for now.

OK, so let's get back to our example and actually run it:

```
$ rbenv shell 1.9.3-p551
$ ruby example_unoptimized.rb
9.18
$ rbenv shell 2.0.0-p598
$ ruby example_unoptimized.rb
11.42
$ rbenv shell 2.1.5
$ ruby example_unoptimized.rb
2.65
$ rbenv shell 2.2.0
$ ruby example_unoptimized.rb
2.43
```

Let's organize the measurements in a tabular format for easy comparison. Further in the book, I'll skip the session printouts and will just include the comparison tables.

	1.9.3	2.0	2.1	2.2
Execution time	9.18	11.42	2.65	2.43

What? Concatenating 100,000 rows, 10 columns each, takes up to 10 seconds? That's way too much. Ruby 2.1 and 2.2 are better, but still take too long. Why is our simple program so slow?

Let's look at our code one more time. It seems like an idiomatic Ruby one-liner that is internally just a loop with a nested loop. The algorithmic efficiency of this code is going to be O(n m) no matter what. So the question is, what can we optimize?

I'll give you a hint. Run this program with garbage collection disabled. For that just add a GC.disable statement before the benchmark block like this:

chp1/example_no_gc.rb
```
require "benchmark"

num_rows = 100000
num_cols = 10
data = Array.new(num_rows) { Array.new(num_cols) { "x"*1000 } }

GC.disable
time = Benchmark.realtime do
  csv = data.map { |row| row.join(",") }.join("\n")
end

puts time.round(2)
```

Now let's run this and compare our measurements with the original program.

	1.9.3	2.0	2.1	2.2
GC enabled	9.18	11.42	2.65	2.43
GC disabled	1.14	1.15	1.19	1.16
% of time spent in GC	88%	90%	55%	52%

Do you see why the code is so slow? Our program spends the majority of its execution time in the garbage collector—a whopping 90% of the time in older Rubys and a significant 50% of the time in modern versions.

I started my career as C++ developer. That's why I was stunned when I first realized how much time Ruby GC takes. This surprises even seasoned developers who have worked with garbage-collected languages like Java and C#. Ruby GC takes as much time as our code itself or more. Yes, Ruby 2.1 and later perform much better. But even they require half the execution time for garbage collection in our example.

What's the deal with the Ruby GC? Did our code use too much memory? Is the Ruby GC too slow? The answer is a resounding yes to both questions.

High memory consumption is intrinsic to Ruby. It's a side effect of the language design. "Everything is an object" means that programs need extra memory to represent data as Ruby objects. Also, slow garbage collection is a well-known historical problem with Ruby. Its mark-and-sweep, stop-the-world GC is not only the slowest known garbage collection algorithm. It also has to stop the application for the time GC is running. That's why our application takes almost a dozen seconds to complete.

You have surely noticed significant performance improvement with Ruby 2.1 and 2.2. These versions feature much improved GC, called restricted generational GC. We'll talk about what that means later in Chapter 10, *Tune Up the Garbage Collector*, on page 149. For now it's important to remember that the latest two Ruby releases are much faster thanks to the better GC.

High GC times are surprising to the uninitiated. Less surprising, but still important, is the fact that without GC all Ruby versions perform the same, finishing in about 1.15 seconds. Internally the Ruby VMs are not that different across the versions starting from 1.9. The biggest improvement relevant to performance is the restricted generational GC that came with Ruby 2.1. But that, of course, has no effect on code performance when GC is disabled.

If you're a Ruby 1.8 user, you shouldn't expect to get the performance of 1.9 and later, even with GC turned off. Modern Rubys have a virtual machine to execute precompiled code. Ruby 1.8 executes code in a much slower fashion by traversing the syntax tree.

OK, let's get back to our example and think about why GC took so much time. What did it do? Well, we know that the more memory we use, the longer GC takes to complete. So we must have allocated a lot of memory, right? Let's see how much by printing memory size before and after our benchmark. The way to do this is to print the process's RSS, or Resident Set Size, which is the portion of a process's memory that's held in RAM.

On Linux and Mac OS X you can get RSS from the ps command:

```
puts "%dM" % `ps -o rss= -p #{Process.pid}`.to_i
```

On Windows your best bet is to use the OS.rss function from the OS gem, https://github.com/rdp/os. The gem is outdated and unmaintained, but it still should work for you.

```
chp1/example_measure_memory.rb
require "benchmark"

num_rows = 100000
num_cols = 10
data = Array.new(num_rows) { Array.new(num_cols) { "x"*1000 } }

➤ puts "%d MB" % (`ps -o rss= -p #{Process.pid}`.to_i/1024)

GC.disable
time = Benchmark.realtime do
  csv = data.map { |row| row.join(",") }.join("\n")
end

➤ puts "%d MB" % (`ps -o rss= -p #{Process.pid}`.to_i/1024)
puts time.round(2)

$ rbenv shell 2.2.0
$ ruby example_measure_memory.rb
1040 MB
2958 MB
```

Aha. Things are getting more and more interesting. Our initial dataset is roughly 1 gigabyte. Here and later in this book when I write kB I mean 1024 bytes, MB - 1024 * 1024 bytes, GB - 1024 * 1024 * 1024 bytes (yes, I know, it's old school). So, we consumed *2 extra gigabytes* of memory to process that 1 GB of data. Your gut feeling is that it should have taken only 1 GB extra. Instead we took 2 GB. No wonder GC has a lot of work to do!

You probably have a bunch of questions already. Why did the program need 2 GB instead of 1 GB? How do we deal with this? Is there a way for our code to use less memory? The answers are in the next section, but first let's review what we've learned so far.

Takeaways

- Memory consumption and garbage collection are among the major reasons why Ruby is slow.

- Ruby has a significant memory overhead.

- GC in Ruby 2.1 and later is up to five times faster than in earlier versions.

- The raw performance of all modern Ruby interpreters is about the same.

Optimize Memory

High memory consumption is what makes Ruby slow. Therefore, to optimize we need to reduce the memory footprint. This will, in turn, reduce the time for garbage collection.

You might ask, why don't we disable GC altogether? That is rarely a good thing to do. Turning off GC significantly increases peak memory consumption. The operating system may run out of memory or start swapping. Both results will hit performance much harder than Ruby GC itself.

So let's get back to our example and think how we can reduce memory consumption. We know that we use 2 GB of memory to process 1 GB of data. So we'll need to look at where that extra memory is used.

```
chp1/example_annotated.rb
require "benchmark"

num_rows = 100000
num_cols = 10
data = Array.new(num_rows) { Array.new(num_cols) { "x"*1000 } }

time = Benchmark.realtime do
  csv = data.map do |row|
    row.join(",")
  end.join("\n")
end

puts time.round(2)
```

I made the map block more verbose to show you where the problem is. The CSV rows that we generate inside that block are actually intermediate results stored into memory until we can finally join them by the newline character. This is exactly where we use that extra 1 GB of memory.

Let's rewrite this in a way that doesn't store any intermediate results. For that I'll explicitly loop over rows with a nested loop over columns and store results as I go into the csv.

```ruby
chp1/example_optimized.rb
require "benchmark"

num_rows = 100000
num_cols = 10
data = Array.new(num_rows) { Array.new(num_cols) { "x"*1000 } }

time = Benchmark.realtime do
  csv = ''
  num_rows.times do |i|
    num_cols.times do |j|
      csv << data[i][j]
      csv << "," unless j == num_cols - 1
    end
    csv << "\n" unless i == num_rows - 1
  end
end

puts time.round(2)
```

The code got uglier, but how fast is it now? Let's run it and compare it with the unoptimized version.

	1.9.3	2.0	2.1	2.2
GC enabled	9.18	11.42	2.65	2.43
GC disabled	1.14	1.15	1.19	1.16
Optimized	1.01	1.06	1.05	1.09

These are great results! Our simple changes got rid of the GC overhead. The optimized program is even faster than the original with no GC. And if you run the optimized version with the GC disabled, you'll find out that its GC time is merely a 10% of total execution time. Because of this, our program performs the same in all Ruby versions.

By making simple changes, we got from 2.5 to 10 times performance improvement. Doing so required us merely to look through the code and think how much memory each line and function call takes. Once you catch memory copying, or extra memory allocation, or another case of a memory-inefficient operation, you rewrite the code to avoid that. Simple, isn't it?

Actually, it is. It turns out that to get significant speedup you might not need code profiling. Memory optimization is easier: just review, think, and rewrite. Only when you are sure that the code spends a reasonable time in GC should

Performance in Ruby 2.1 and Later

It turns out Ruby 2.1 is not a silver performance bullet. It indeed speeds up unopti-mized code, but memory-efficient code actually nets no improvement from Ruby 2.1. *Once your program is memory optimized, it doesn't matter much which Ruby version you run.* You will always get the best possible performance.

My personal experience is that 2.1 and 2.2 finally make *default* Ruby application performance acceptable, on par with other dynamic programming languages. This is the level of performance that you'd probably expect these days. But it's nothing spectacular, and it still requires optimization.

you look further and try to locate algorithmic complexity or other sources of poor performance.

But in my experience there's often no need to optimize anything other than memory. For me the following 80-20 rule of Ruby performance optimization is always true: 80% of performance improvements come from memory opti-mization, the remaining 20% from everything else.

Review, think, and rewrite. Maybe we should think about thinking. If optimiz-ing memory requires rethinking what the code does, then what exactly should we think about? We'll talk about that in the next section, but first let's review what we've learned so far.

Takeaways

- The 80-20 rule of Ruby performance optimization: 80% of performance improvements come from memory optimization, so optimize memory first.

- A memory-optimized program has the same performance in any modern Ruby versions.

- Ruby 2.1 is not a silver performance bullet; it just minimizes losses.

Get Into the Performance Mind-set

Ruby optimization is more about rethinking what the code does and less about finding bottlenecks with specialized tools. The major skill to learn is rather the right way of thinking about performance. This is what I call the Ruby Performance Mind-set.

How do you get into this mind-set? Let me give you a hint. When you write code, remember that memory consumption and garbage collection are, most likely, why Ruby is slow, and constantly ask yourself these three questions:

1. Is Ruby the right tool to solve my problem?

   Ruby is a general-purpose programming language, but that doesn't mean you should use it to solve all your problems. There are things that Ruby is not so good at. The prime example is large dataset processing. That needs memory: exactly the sort of thing that you want to avoid.

   This task is better done in a database or in background processes written in other programming languages. Twitter, for example, once had a Ruby on Rails front end backed by Scala workers. Another example is statistical computations, which are better done with, say, the R language.

2. How much memory will my code use?

   The less memory your code uses, the less work Ruby GC has to do. You already know some tricks to reduce memory consumption—the ones that we used in our example: line-by-line data processing and avoiding intermediate objects. I'll show you more in subsequent chapters.

3. What is the raw performance of this code?

   Once you're sure the memory is used optimally, take a look at the algorithmic complexity of the code itself.

Asking these three questions, in the stated order, will get you into the Ruby Performance Mind-set. And then you may begin to find that new code that you write is fast right from the start, without any optimization required.

Ah, but what can you do about an old program? What problems should you look for? It turns out that the majority of performance problems come from a relatively limited number of sources. In the next chapter we'll talk about these, and how to fix them.

## CHAPTER 2

Fix Common Performance Problems

There is nothing new under the sun.

The reasons code is slow invariably come down to familiar issues. This is especially true for us Ruby developers. We are far removed from writing bare-metal code. We heavily use language features, standard libraries, gems, and frameworks. And each of these brings along its performance issues. Some of these are actually memory inefficient by design! We should be extremely careful about how we write our code and what features or libraries we use.

We have talked about two of the common reasons for poor performance in the previous chapter: extra memory allocation and data structure copying. What are the others?

Execution context copying, memory-heavy iterators, slow type conversions, and iterator-unsafe functions are a few of the culprits. In the next pages I'll walk you through the steps to avoid these. But before we start, let's briefly talk about a subject we've avoided so far: measurements.

We need some way to know that the changes we make really improve performance. In the previous chapter we used Benchmark.realtime to measure execution time and `ps -o rss= -p #{Process.pid}`.to_i to measure current memory usage. To understand how reduced memory usage translates into the improved performance, we'll also measure the number of GC calls and the time required for GC. The former is easy to measure. Ruby provides the GC#stat function that returns the number of GC runs (and more stats that we'll ignore for now). The latter is harder, and requires running the same program twice, once with GC disabled, and getting a difference you can attribute to GC.

Let's build a tool. We'll create a wrapper function that will measure execution time, the number of GC runs, and total allocated memory. In addition to that, let's make the function read the --no-gc command-line option and turn off GC if requested.

chp2/wrapper.rb

```ruby
require "json"
require "benchmark"

def measure(&block)
  no_gc = (ARGV[0] == "--no-gc")

  if no_gc
    GC.disable
  else
    # collect memory allocated during library loading
    # and our own code before the measurement
    GC.start
  end

  memory_before = `ps -o rss= -p #{Process.pid}`.to_i/1024
  gc_stat_before = GC.stat
  time = Benchmark.realtime do
    yield
  end
  puts ObjectSpace.count_objects
  unless no_gc
    GC.start(full_mark: true, immediate_sweep: true, immediate_mark: false)
  end
  puts ObjectSpace.count_objects
  gc_stat_after = GC.stat
  memory_after = `ps -o rss= -p #{Process.pid}`.to_i/1024

  puts({
    RUBY_VERSION => {
      gc: no_gc ? 'disabled' : 'enabled',
      time: time.round(2),
      gc_count: gc_stat_after[:count] - gc_stat_before[:count],
      memory: "%d MB" % (memory_after - memory_before)
    }
  }.to_json)
end
```

OK, there's another way to measure GC time: the GC::Profiler that Ruby 1.9.2 introduced. The problem is that it adds significant overhead to both memory and CPU. This is good for profiling where absolute numbers are not important and you're interested only in relative values. It's less useful for measurements that we want to do in this chapter.

Memory measurements with and without GC will of course differ. In the former case, we will get the amount of memory allocated by the block that stays allocated after we're done. We'll use this number to find memory leaks. In the latter case, we'll get total memory consumption: the amount of memory allocated during the execution of the block. That's the metric we'll use most often in this chapter, as it directly shows how much work your program makes for the GC.

So let's do some measuring. Let's use the wrapper to run our unoptimized code example from the previous chapter. Here and later in this chapter I will use Ruby 2.2 to run my examples unless otherwise noted.

chp2/wrapper_example.rb
```ruby
require 'wrapper'
require 'csv'

measure do
  data = CSV.open("data.csv")
  output = data.readlines.map do |line|
    line.map { |col| col.downcase.gsub(/\b('?[a-z])/) { $1.capitalize } }
  end
  File.open("output.csv", "w+") { |f| f.write output.join("\n") }
end
```

```
$ cd code/chp2
$ ruby -I . wrapper_example.rb
{"2.2.0":{"gc":"enabled","time":14.96,"gc_count":27,"memory":"479 MB"}}
$ ruby -I . wrapper_example.rb --no-gc
{"2.2.0":{"gc":"disabled","time":10.17,"gc_count":0,"memory":"1555 MB"}}
```

The results are exactly what we saw before. But in addition, we see that GC kicked off 27 times during execution. As usual with these measurements, you will have to run the wrapper several times to obtain (more or less) accurate measurement. But there's no need yet to aim for statistical significance. We'll handle that problem later.

So let's take this wrapper as a basic measurement tool and see what is slow in Ruby and how to fix it.

Save Memory

The first step to make your application faster is to save memory. Every time you create or copy something in memory, you add work for GC. Let's look at the best practices to write code that doesn't use too much memory.

Modify Strings in Place

Ruby programs use a lot of strings, and copy them a lot. In most cases they really shouldn't. You can do most string manipulations in place, meaning that instead of making a changed copy, you change the original.

Ruby has a bunch of "bang!" functions for in-place modification. Those are gsub!, capitalize!, downcase!, upcase!, delete!, reverse!, slice!, and others. It's always a good idea to use them as much as you can when you no longer need the original string.

```
chp2/string_in_place1.rb
Line 1  require 'wrapper'
     2
     3  str = "X" * 1024 * 1024 * 10     # 10 MB string
     4  measure do
     5    str = str.downcase
     6  end
     7  measure do
     8    str.downcase!
     9  end
```

```
$ ruby -I . string_in_place1.rb --no-gc
{"2.2.0":{"gc":"disabled","time":0.02,"gc_count":0,"memory":"9 MB"}}
{"2.2.0":{"gc":"disabled","time":0.01,"gc_count":0,"memory":"0 MB"}}
```

The String#downcase call on line 5 allocates another 10 MB in memory to copy a string, then changes it to lowercase. The bang version of the same function on line 8 does not need any extra memory. And that's exactly what we see in the measurements.

Another useful in-place modification function is String::<<. It concatenates strings by appending a new string to the original. When asked to append one string to another, most developers write this:

```
x = "foo"
x += "bar"
```

This code is equivalent to

```
x = "foo"
y = x + "bar"
x = y
```

Here Ruby allocates extra memory to store the result of the concatenation. The same code using the shift operator will need no additional memory if your resulting string is less than 40 bytes (on a 64-bit architecture; more on that later on page 149). If the string is larger than that, Ruby will only allocate enough memory to store the appended string. So next time, write this instead:

```
x = "foo"
x << "bar"
```

Behind the scenes the String#<< may not be able to increase the size of the original string to do a true in-place modification. In this case it may have to move the string data in memory into the new location. However, that happens in the realloc() C library function behind Ruby's back and does not trigger GC.

Another thing worth pointing out is that "bang!" functions are not guaranteed to do an in-place modification. Most of them do, but that's implementation dependent. So don't be surprised when one of them doesn't optimize anything.

Modify Arrays and Hashes in Place

Like strings, arrays and hashes can be modified in place. If you look at the Ruby API documentation, you'll again see "bang!" functions like map!, select!, reject!, and others. The idea is the same: do not create a modified copy of the same array unless really necessary.

String, array, and hash in-place modification functions are extremely powerful when used together. Compare these two examples:

chp2/combined_in_place1.rb
```
require 'wrapper'

data = Array.new(100) { "x" * 1024 * 1024 }

measure do
  data.map { |str| str.upcase }
end
```

chp2/combined_in_place2.rb
```
require 'wrapper'

data = Array.new(100) { "x" * 1024 * 1024 }

measure do
  data.map! { |str| str.upcase! }
end
```

	map and upcase	map! and upcase!
Total time	0.22 s	0.14 s
Extra memory	100 MB	0 MB
# of GC calls	3	0

See how this code got 35% faster by simply adding two "!" characters? Easy optimization, isn't it? The second example gives no work to GC at all despite crunching through 100 MB of data.

Read Files Line by Line

It takes memory to read the whole file. We expect that, of course, and sometimes willingly do that for convenience. But as usual with Ruby, it takes a toll on memory. How big is the overhead? It's insignificant if you just read the file. For example, reading the 26 MB data.csv file[1] takes exactly 26 MB of memory.

chp2/file_reading1.rb

```
require 'wrapper'
measure do
  File.read("data.csv")
end
```

```
$ ruby -I . file_reading1.rb --no-gc
{"2.2.0":{"gc":"disabled","time":0.02,"gc_count":0,"memory":"25 MB"}}
```

Here we simply create one File object (it takes just 40 bytes on a 64-bit architecture) and store the 26 MB string there. No extra memory is used.

Things rapidly become less perfect when we try to parse the file. For example, it takes 158 MB to split the same CSV file into lines and columns.

chp2/file_reading2.rb

```
require 'wrapper'
measure do
  File.readlines("data.csv").map! { |line| line.split(",") }
end
```

```
$ ruby -I . file_reading2.rb --no-gc
{"2.2.0":{"gc":"disabled","time":0.45,"gc_count":0,"memory":"186 MB"}}
```

What does Ruby use this memory for? The file has about 163,000 rows of data in 11 columns. So, to store the parsed contents we should allocate 163,000 objects for rows and 1,793,000 objects for columns—1,956,000 objects in total. On a 64-bit architecture that requires approximately 75 MB. Together with 26 MB necessary to read the file, our program needs at least 101 MB of memory. In addition to that, not all strings are small enough to fit into 40-byte Ruby objects. Ruby will allocate more memory to store them. That's what the remaining 85 MB are used for. As the result, our simple program takes seven times the size of our data after parsing.

The Ruby CSV parser takes even more. It needs 346 MB of memory, 13 times the data size.

---

1. http://www.cms.gov/Research-Statistics-Data-and-Systems/Statistics-Trends-and-Reports/Medicare-Provider-Charge-Data/Downloads/IPPS_DRG_CSV.zip

```
chp2/file_reading3.rb
require 'wrapper'
require 'csv'

measure do
  CSV.read("data.csv")
end
```

```
$ ruby -I . file_reading3.rb --no-gc
{"2.2.0":{"gc":"disabled","time":2.66,"gc_count":0,"memory":"368 MB"}}
```

This memory consumption math is really disturbing. In my experience, the size of the data after parsing increases anywhere from two up to ten times depending on the nature of the data in real-world applications. That's a lot of work for Ruby GC.

The solution? Read and parse data files line by line as much as possible. In the previous chapter we did that for the CSV file and got a two times speedup.

Whenever you can, read files line by line, as in this example:

```
chp2/file_reading4.rb
require 'wrapper'

measure do
  file = File.open("data.csv", "r")
  while line = file.gets
    line.split(",")
  end
end
```

And do the same with CSV files:

```
chp2/file_reading5.rb
require 'csv'
require 'wrapper'

measure do
  file = CSV.open("data.csv")
  while line = file.readline
  end
end
```

Now, let's measure these examples with our wrapper code. To our surprise, memory allocation is about the same as before: 171 MB and 367 MB.

```
$ ruby -I . file_reading4.rb --no-gc
{"2.2.0":{"gc":"disabled","time":0.45,"gc_count":0,"memory":"171 MB"}}
$ ruby -I . file_reading5.rb --no-gc
{"2.2.0":{"gc":"disabled","time":2.64,"gc_count":0,"memory":"367 MB"}}
```

But if you think about this a little more, you'll understand. It doesn't matter how we parse the file—in one go, or line by line. We'll end up allocating the same amount of memory anyway. And look at execution time. It's the same as before. What's the deal?

We've been measuring the total amount of memory allocated. That makes sense when we want to know exactly how much memory in total a certain snippet of code needs. *But it doesn't tell us anything about peak memory consumption.* During program execution, GC will deallocate unused memory. This will reduce both peak memory consumption and GC time because there's much less data held in memory at any given moment.

When we read a file line by line, we're telling Ruby that we don't need the previous lines anymore. GC will then collect them as your program executes. So, to see the optimization, you need to turn on GC. Let's do that and compare before and after numbers.

Before optimization:

```
$ ruby -I . file_reading2.rb
{"2.2.0":{"gc":"enabled","time":0.68,"gc_count":11,"memory":"144 MB"}}
$ ruby -I . file_reading3.rb
{"2.2.0":{"gc":"enabled","time":3.25,"gc_count":17,"memory":"175 MB"}}
```

After optimization:

```
$ ruby -I . file_reading4.rb
{"2.2.0":{"gc":"enabled","time":0.44,"gc_count":106,"memory":"0 MB"}}
$ ruby -I . file_reading5.rb
{"2.2.0":{"gc":"enabled","time":2.62,"gc_count":246,"memory":"1 MB"}}
```

Now you see why reading files line by line is such a good idea. First, you'll end up using almost no additional memory. In fact, you'll end up storing just the line you are processing and any previous lines that were allocated after the last GC call. Second, the program will run faster. Speedup depends on the data size; in our examples it is 35% for plain file reading and 20% for CSV parsing.

Watch for Memory Leaks Caused by Callbacks

Rails developers know and use callbacks a lot. But when done wrong, callbacks can hurt performance. For example, let's write a logger object that will lazily record object creation. For that, instead of writing the output right away, it will log events and replay them later all at once. It is tempting to implement the event logger using Ruby closures (lambdas or Procs) like this:

Joe asks:

Optimized CSV Parsing Example Runs GC Way More Often but Still Finishes Faster. What Gives?

Ruby 2.2 has incremental garbage collection that runs more often, but collects only a small part of object space. That's why you see several hundreds of GC runs. For our example this works best, as GC runs once per about 1,600 rows processed (163,000 rows divided by 106 collections in the plain file parsing example). This amounts to only 260k of additional memory needed for the parsing at any given moment during the program execution. Our example reports 0 MB of additional memory because it does the rounding.

The math will be different for older Rubys, but expect the end result to be similar. You will see the optimization with any Ruby version. Go check it yourself!

chp2/callbacks1.rb
```ruby
module Logger
  extend self
  attr_accessor :output, :log_actions

  def log(&event)
    self.log_actions ||= []
    self.log_actions << event
  end

  def play
    output = []
    log_actions.each { |e| e.call(output) }
    puts output.join("\n")
  end
end

class Thing
  def initialize(id)
    Logger.log { |output| output << "created thing #{id}" }
  end
end

def do_something
  1000.times { |i| Thing.new(i) }
end

do_something
GC.start
Logger.play
puts ObjectSpace.each_object(Thing).count
```

We log an event by storing a block of code that gets executed later. The code actually looks quite cool. At least I feel cool every time I use bits of functional programming in Ruby.

Unfortunately, when I write something cool or smart, it tends to turn out slow and inefficient. The same thing happens here. Such logging will keep the references to all created objects even if we don't need them. So add the following lines to the end of the program and run it:

```
GC.start  # collect all unused objects
puts ObjectSpace.each_object(Thing).count
```

```
$ ruby -I . callbacks1.rb
created thing 0
created thing 1
«...»
created thing 999
1000
```

After we're done with the do_something, we don't really need all one thousand of these Thing objects. But even an explicit GC.start call does not collect them. What's going on?

Callbacks stored in the Logger class are the reason the objects are still there. When you pass an anonymous block in the Thing constructor to the Logger#log function, Ruby converts it into the Proc object and stores references to all objects in the block's execution context. That includes the Thing instance. In this way we end up keeping references from the Logger object to all one thousand instances of Thing. It's a classic example of a memory leak.

A dumbed-down version of the Logger class will look less cool, but will prevent the memory leak. You can of course write an even more dumb version that doesn't use any callbacks at all, but I'll keep them for this example.

chp2/callbacks2.rb
```ruby
module Logger
  extend self
  attr_accessor :output

  def log(&event)
    self.output ||= []
    event.call(output)
  end

  def play
    puts output.join("\n")
  end
end
```

```ruby
class Thing
  def initialize(id)
    Logger.log { |output| output << "created thing #{id}" }
  end
end

def do_something
  1000.times { |i| Thing.new(i) }
end

do_something
GC.start
Logger.play
puts ObjectSpace.each_object(Thing).count
```

```
$ ruby -I . callbacks1.rb
created thing 0
created thing 1
«...»
created thing 999
0
```

In this case no memory is leaked and all Thing objects are garbage collected.

So be careful every time you create a block or Proc callback. Remember, if you store it somewhere, you will also keep references to its execution context. That not only hurts the performance, but also might even leak memory.

Are All Anonymous Blocks Dangerous to Performance?

Anonymous blocks do not store execution context unless they are converted to Proc objects. When calling a function that takes an anonymous block, Ruby stores a reference to the caller's stack frame. It's OK to do that since the callee is guaranteed to exit before the caller's stack frame is popped. When calling a function that takes a named block, Ruby assumes that this block is long-lived and clones the execution context right there.

An obvious case of anonymous block to Proc conversion is when your receiving function defines the &block argument.

```ruby
def take_block(&block)
  block.call(args)
end
take_block { |args| do_something(args) }
```

It's a good idea to change such code to use anonymous blocks. We don't really need the Proc conversion since the block is simply executed, and never stored as in the logger example in the previous section.

```
def take_block
  yield(args)
end
take_block { |args| do_something(args) }
```

However, it's not always clear when conversion happens. It may be hidden well down into the call stack, or even happen in C code inside the Ruby interpreter. Let's look at this example:

```
chp2/signal1.rb
Line 1  class LargeObject
   -      def initialize
   -        @data = "x" * 1024 * 1024 * 20
   -      end
   5    end

   -    def do_something
   -      obj = LargeObject.new
   -      trap("TERM") { puts obj.inspect }
  10    end

   -    do_something
   -    # force major GC to make sure we free all objects that can be freed
   -    GC.start(full_mark: true, immediate_sweep: true)
  15    puts "LargeObject instances left in memory: %d" %
   -      ObjectSpace.each_object(LargeObject).count
```

```
$ ruby -I . signal1.rb
LargeObject instances left in memory: 1
```

This example behaves suspiciously similar to what we saw with the smart logger in the previous section. It leaves one large object behind. There's only one place in the code that could cause that. Line 9 passes an anonymous block to the trap function. A quick look at the source code[2] reveals that the trap implementation calls cmd = rb_block_proc(); that indeed converts the block to Proc behind the scenes.

If you comment out line 9, the program will report 0 large objects left after execution.

So, if you suspect memory leaks in named blocks, you'll have to review the code down the stack—at least down to the Ruby standard library, including functions implemented in C. It's not as hard as it sounds. You can always look up the function implementation in the Ruby API docs from the website. Ruby source code is well written and clean. You'll be able to make sense of it even if you don't know any C, as with the trap example earlier.

---

2.   http://www.ruby-doc.org/core-2.1.2/Signal.html#method-c-trap

Optimize Your Iterators

To a Ruby newcomer, Ruby iterators typically look like a convenient syntax for loops. In fact, iterators are such a good abstraction that even seasoned developers often forget that they really are nothing more than methods of Array and Hash classes with a block argument.

However, keeping this in mind is important for performance. We talked in *Modify Arrays and Hashes in Place*, on page 17 about the importance of in-place operations on hashes and arrays. But that's not the end of the story.

Because a Ruby iterator is a function of an object (Array, Range, Hash, etc.), it has two characteristics that affect performance:

1. Ruby GC will not garbage collect the object you're iterating before the iterator is finished. This means that when you have a large list in memory, that whole list will stay in memory even if you no longer need the parts you've already traversed.

2. Iterators, being functions, can and will create temporary objects behind the scenes. This adds work for the garbage collector and hurts performance.

Compounding these performance hits, iterators (just like loops) are sensitive to the algorithmic complexity of the code. An operation that by itself is just a tad slow becomes a huge time sink when repeated hundreds of thousands of times.

So let's see when exactly iterators become slow and what can we do about that.

Free Objects from Collections During Iteration

Let's assume we have a list of objects, say one thousand elements of class Thing. We iterate over the list, do something useful, and discard the list. I've seen and written a lot of such code in production applications. For example, you read data from a file, calculate some stats, and return only the stats.

```ruby
class Thing; end
list = Array.new(1000) { Thing.new }

list.each do |item|
  # do something with the item
end
list = nil
```

Obviously we can't deallocate list before each finishes. So it will stay in memory even if we no longer need access to previously traversed items. Let's prove that by counting the number of Thing instances before each iteration.

chp2/each_bang.rb

```
class Thing; end
list = Array.new(1000) { Thing.new }
puts ObjectSpace.each_object(Thing).count # 1000 objects

list.each do |item|
  GC.start
  puts ObjectSpace.each_object(Thing).count # same count as before
  # do something with the item
end

list = nil
GC.start
puts ObjectSpace.each_object(Thing).count # everything has been deallocated

$ ruby -I . each_bang.rb
1000
1000
«...»
1000
1000
0
```

As expected, only when we clear the list reference does the whole list get garbage collected. We can do better by using a while loop and removing elements from the list as we process them, like this:

chp2/each_bang.rb

```
class Thing; end
list = Array.new(1000) { Thing.new }   # allocate 1000 objects again
puts ObjectSpace.each_object(Thing).count

while list.count > 0
  GC.start     # this will garbage collect item from previous iteration
  puts ObjectSpace.each_object(Thing).count # watch the counter decreasing
  item = list.shift
end

GC.start     # this will garbage collect item from previous iteration
puts ObjectSpace.each_object(Thing).count # watch the counter decreasing

$ ruby -I . each_bang.rb
1000
999
«...»
2
1
```

See how the object counter decreases as we loop through the list? I'm again running GC before each iteration to show you that all previous elements are garbage and will be collected. In the real world you wouldn't want to force GC. Just let it do its job and your loop will neither take too much time nor run out of memory.

Don't worry about negative effects of list modification inside the loop. GC time savings will outweight them if you process lots of objects. That happens both when your list is large and when you load linked data from these objects—for example, Rails associations.

Use the Each! Pattern

If we wrap our loop that removes items from an array during iteration into a Ruby iterator, we'll get what its creator, Alexander Goldstein, called "Each!". This is how the simplest each! iterator looks:

chp2/each_bang_pattern.rb
```
class Array
  def each!
    while count > 0
      yield(shift)
    end
  end
end

Array.new(10000).each! { |element| puts element.class }
```

This implementation is not 100% idiomatic Ruby because it doesn't return an Enumerator if there's no block passed. But it illustrates the concept well enough. Also note how it avoids creating Proc objects from anonymous blocks (there's no &block argument).

Avoid Iterators That Create Additional Objects

It turns out that some Ruby iterators (not all of them as we will see) internally create additional Ruby objects. Compare these two examples:

chp2/iterator_each1.rb
```
GC.disable
before = ObjectSpace.count_objects

Array.new(10000).each do |i|
  [0,1].each do |j|
  end
end

after = ObjectSpace.count_objects
```

```
puts "# of arrays: %d" % (after[:T_ARRAY] - before[:T_ARRAY])
puts "# of nodes: %d" % (after[:T_NODE] - before[:T_NODE])
```

```
$ ruby -I . iterator_each1.rb
# of arrays: 10001
# of nodes: 0
```

chp2/iterator_each2.rb
```
GC.disable
before = ObjectSpace.count_objects

Array.new(10000).each do |i|
  [0,1].each_with_index do |j, index|
  end
end

after = ObjectSpace.count_objects
puts "# of arrays: %d" % (after[:T_ARRAY] - before[:T_ARRAY])
puts "# of nodes: %d" % (after[:T_NODE] - before[:T_NODE])
```

```
$ ruby -I . iterator_each2.rb
# of arrays: 10001
# of nodes: 20000
```

As you'd expect, the code creates 10,000 temporary [0,1] arrays. But something fishy is going on with the number of T_NODE objects. Why would each_with_index create 20,000 extra objects?

The answer is in the Ruby source code. Here's the implementation of each:

```
VALUE
rb_ary_each(VALUE array)
{
    long i;
    volatile VALUE ary = array;
    RETURN_SIZED_ENUMERATOR(ary, 0, 0, ary_enum_length);
    for (i=0; i<RARRAY_LEN(ary); i++) {
        rb_yield(RARRAY_AREF(ary, i));
    }
    return ary;
}
```

Compare it to the implementation of and each_with_index.

```
enum_each_with_index(int argc, VALUE *argv, VALUE obj)
{
    NODE *memo;
    RETURN_SIZED_ENUMERATOR(obj, argc, argv, enum_size);
    memo = NEW_MEMO(0, 0, 0);
    rb_block_call(obj, id_each, argc, argv, each_with_index_i, (VALUE)memo);
    return obj;
}
```

```
static VALUE
each_with_index_i(RB_BLOCK_CALL_FUNC_ARGLIST(i, memo))
{
    long n = RNODE(memo)->u3.cnt++;
    return rb_yield_values(2, rb_enum_values_pack(argc, argv), INT2NUM(n));
}
```

Even if your C-fu is not that strong, you'll still see that each_with_index creates an additional NODE *memo variable. Because our each_with_index loop is nested in another loop, we get to create 10,000 additional nodes. Worse, the internal function each_with_index_i allocates one more node. Thus we end up with the 20,000 extra T_NODE objects that you see in our example output.

How does that affect performance? Imagine your nested loop is executed not 10,000 times, but 1 million times. You'll get 2 million objects created. And while they can be freed during the iteration, GC still gets way too much work to do. How's that for an iterator that you would otherwise easily mistake for a syntactic construct?

It would be nice to know which iterators are bad for performance and which are not, wouldn't it? I thought so, and so I calculated the number of additional T_NODE objects created per iterator. The table on page 30 summarizes the results for commonly used iterators.

Iterators that create 0 additional objects are safe to use in nested loops. But be careful with those that allocate two or even three additional objects: all?, each_with_index, inject, and others.

Looking at the table, we can also spot that iterators of the Array class, and in some cases the Hash class, behave differently. It turns out that Range and Hash use default iterator implementations from the Enumerable module, while Array reimplements most of them. That not only results in better algorithmical performance (that was the reason behind the reimplementation), but also in better memory consumption. This means that most of Array's iterators are safe to use, with the notable exceptions of each_with_index and inject.

Watch for Iterator-Unsafe Ruby Standard Library Functions

Iterators are where the algorithmic complexity of the functions you use matters, even in Ruby. One millisecond lost in a loop with one thousand iterations translates to a one-second slowdown. Let me show which commonly used Ruby functions are slow and how to replace them with faster analogs.

Iterator	Enum†	Array	Range	Iterator	Enum†	Array	Range
all?	3	3	3	fill	0	—	—
any?	2	2	2	find	2	2	2
collect	0	1	1	find_all	1	1	1
cycle	0	1	1	grep	2	2	2
delete_if	0	—	0	inject	2	2	2
detect	2	2	2	map	0	1	1
each	0	0	0	none?	2	2	2
each_index	0	—	—	one?	2	2	2
each_key	—	—	0	reduce	2	2	2
each_pair	—	—	0	reject	0	1	0
each_value	—	—	0	reverse	0	—	—
each_with_index	2	2	2	reverse_each	0	1	1
each_with_object	1	1	1	select	0	1	0

Table 1—Number of additional T_NODE objects created by an iterator

† Enum is Enumerable

Date#parse

Date parsing in Ruby has been traditionally slow, but this function is especially harmful for performance. Let's see how much time it uses in a loop with 100,000 iterations:

```
chp2/date_parsing1.rb
require 'date'
require 'benchmark'

date = "2014-05-23"
time = Benchmark.realtime do
  100000.times do
    Date.parse(date)
  end
end
puts "%.3f" % time
```

```
$ ruby date_parsing1.rb
0.833
```

Each Date#parse call takes a minuscule 0.02 ms. But in a moderately large loop, that translates into almost one second of execution time.

A better solution is to let the date parser know which date format to use, like this:

```
chp2/date_parsing2.rb
require 'date'
require 'benchmark'

date = "2014-05-23"
time = Benchmark.realtime do
  100000.times do
    Date.strptime(date, '%Y-%m-%d')
  end
end
puts "%.3f" % time
```

```
$ ruby date_parsing2.rb
0.182
```

That is already 4.6 times faster. But avoiding date string parsing altogether is even faster:

```
chp2/date_parsing3.rb
require 'date'
require 'benchmark'

date = "2014-05-23"
time = Benchmark.realtime do
  100000.times do
    Date.civil(date[0,4].to_i, date[5,2].to_i, date[8,2].to_i)
  end
end
puts "%.3f" % time
```

```
$ ruby date_parsing3.rb
0.108
```

While slightly uglier, that code is almost eight times faster than the original, and almost two times faster than the Date#strptime version.

Object#class, Object#is_a?, Object#kind_of?

These have considerable performance overhead when used in loops or frequently used functions like constructors or == comparison operators.

```
chp2/class_check1.rb
require 'benchmark'

obj = "sample string"
time = Benchmark.realtime do
  100000.times do
    obj.class == String
  end
end
puts time
```

```
$ ruby class_check1.rb
0.022767841
```

chp2/class_check2.rb
```
require 'benchmark'

obj = "sample string"
time = Benchmark.realtime do
  100000.times do
    obj.is_a?(String)
  end
end
puts time
```

```
$ ruby class_check2.rb
0.019568893
```

In a moderately large loop, again 100,000 iterations, such checks take 19–22 ms. That doesn't sound bad, except that, for example, a Rails application can call comparison operators more than 1 million times per request and spend longer than 200 ms doing type checks.

It's a good idea to move type checking away from iterators or frequently called functions and operators. If you can't, unfortunately there's not much you can do about that.

BigDecimal::==(String)

Code that gets data from databases uses big decimals a lot. That is especially true for Rails applications. Such code often creates a BigDecimal from a string that it reads from a database, and then compares it directly with strings.

The catch is that the natural way to do this comparison is unbelievably slow in Ruby version 1.9.3 and lower:

chp2/bigdecimal1.rb
```
require 'bigdecimal'
require 'benchmark'

x = BigDecimal("10.2")
time = Benchmark.realtime do
  100000.times do
    x == "10.2"
  end
end
puts time
```

```
$ rbenv shell 1.9.3-p551
$ ruby bigdecimal1.rb
0.773866128
```

```
$ rbenv shell 2.0.0-p598
$ ruby bigdecimal1.rb
0.025224029
$ rbenv shell 2.1.5
$ ruby bigdecimal1.rb
0.027570681
$ rbenv shell 2.2.0
$ ruby bigdecimal1.rb
0.02474011096637696
```

Older Rubys have unacceptably slow implementations of the BigDecimal::== function. This performance problem goes away with a Ruby 2.0 upgrade. But if you can't upgrade, use this smart trick. Convert a BigDecimal to a String before comparison:

chp2/bigdecimal2.rb
```ruby
require 'bigdecimal'
require 'benchmark'

x = BigDecimal("10.2")
time = Benchmark.realtime do
  100000.times do
    x.to_s == "10.2"
  end
end
puts time
```

```
$ rbenv shell 1.9.3-p545
$ ruby bigdecimal2.rb
0.195041792
```

This hack is three to four times faster—not forty times faster, as in the Ruby 2.x implementation, but still an improvement.

Write Less Ruby

One of the gurus who taught me programming used to say that the best code is the code that does not exist. If we could solve the problem without writing any code, then we wouldn't have to optimize it. Right?

Unfortunately, in the real world we still write code to solve our problems. But that doesn't mean that it has to be Ruby code. Other tools do certain things better. We have seen that Ruby is especially bad in two areas: large dataset processing and complex computations. So let's see what you can use instead, and how that improves performance.

Offload Work to the Database

The Ruby community tends to view databases only as data storage tools. Rails developers are especially prone to this because they often use ActiveRecord and ActiveModel abstractions without having to interface with the database directly. So yes, you can build a Rails application without knowing any SQL or understanding the differences between MySQL and PostgreSQL. But by doing this, you'll trade performance for convenience and miss out on the data processing power that databases provide.

It turns out—surprise, surprise—that databases are really good at complex computations and other kinds of data manipulation. Let me show you just how good they are.

Let's imagine we have a large database with company employees, say, 10,000 people working in 25 various departments. We know each person's salary, and we want to to calculate the employees' rank within a department by salary.

I'll use PostgreSQL for this example and will create random data for simplicity. To reproduce this example, you should install and launch the PostgreSQL database server.

```
$ createdb company_data
$ psql company_data

create table empsalaries(
  department_id integer,
  employee_id integer,
  salary integer);

insert into empsalaries (
  select (1 + round(random()*25)), *, (50000 + round(random()*250000))
    from generate_series(1, 10000)
);

create index empsalaries_department_id_idx on empsalaries (department_id);
```

Let me explain this in case you're not familiar with PostgreSQL. The insert statement will generate a series of 10,000 rows (our employee IDs), and then for each of those rows will assign a random department ID from 1 to 25 and a random salary from $50,000 to $250,000.

Let's first use ActiveRecord to calculate an employee rank. For that we'll create a folder called group_rank with Gemfile and group_rank.rb in it.

chp2/group_rank/Gemfile

```
source 'https://rubygems.org'

gem 'activerecord'
gem 'pg'
```

chp2/group_rank/group_rank.rb

```
require 'rubygems'
require 'active_record'

ActiveRecord::Base.establish_connection(
  :adapter  => "postgresql",
  :database => "company_data"
)

class Empsalary < ActiveRecord::Base
  attr_accessor :rank
end

time = Benchmark.realtime do
  salaries = Empsalary.all.order(:department_id, :salary)

  key, counter = nil, nil
  salaries.each do |s|
    if s.department_id != key
      key, counter = s.department_id, 0
    end
    counter += 1
    s.rank = counter
  end
end

puts "Group rank with ActiveRecord: %5.3fs" % time
```

Now let's run bundler to install all the required gems and launch the application to see how long it takes to execute:

```
$ cd group_rank
$ rbenv shell 2.2.0
$ bundle install --path .bundle/gems
$ bundle exec ruby group_rank.rb
Group rank with ActiveRecord: 0.264s
```

Taking 246 ms to process a mere 10,000 rows is pretty bad. Now try to do the same thing with 100,000 rows and 1 million rows. Ruby >= 2.0 will take 2.4 and 24 seconds, respectively. Older Rubys like 1.8 and 1.9 might not even finish because GC will kick in too often. I was patient enough to wait 110 seconds for Ruby 1.9 to process 1 million rows. I'm quite sure the users of my code are not that patient.

Now let's see how fast PostgreSQL can do the same thing on 10,000 rows:

```
$ psql company_data
```

```
=# \timing
Timing is on.
=# select department_id, employee_id, salary,
      rank() over(partition by department_id order by salary desc)
   from empsalaries;
Time: 22.573 ms
```

This is ten times faster in PostgreSQL. As a bonus, it also scales nicely. It needs 280 ms for 100,000 rows and 2.3 seconds for 1 million rows.

Notice how PostgreSQL's performance is consistently ten times faster than the best of Ruby's. Yes, my example uses Postgres-specific features like window functions. But that's exactly my point. The database is much better at data processing. That makes a huge difference. We have seen that ten times is not a limit. Sometimes it's a difference between never finishing the task in Ruby and completing it in several seconds simply by letting your database do what it's good at.

Rewrite in C

Ruby is implemented in C, so it has an easy way to interface with C code. So if your Ruby code is slow, you can always rewrite it in C. Wait! What? Fear not, I'm not going to try to talk you into writing the C code yourself. You can certainly do that, but it's out of the scope of this book. Instead I'd like to point out that there are plenty of Ruby gems written in C that do the job faster than their counterparts.

I divide these native code gems into two types:

1. Gems that rewrite slow parts of Ruby or Ruby on Rails in C

2. Gems that implement a specific task in C

The Date::Performance gem[3] is a good example of the first type. It's an old gem that all Ruby 1.8 developers should use. It transparently replaces the slow Ruby Date and DateTime libraries with a similar implementation written in C.

Note that the Date::Performance gem is Ruby 1.8 only. Ruby 1.9 and later have a date library that is much faster.

---

3.   https://github.com/rtomayko/date-performance

Let me show how much faster Date::Performance is. For that, we'll switch to Ruby 1.8, install the date-performance gem, and measure the execution time (without GC, to factor it out) of a program that creates a lot of Date objects.

```
$ rbenv shell 1.8.7-p375
$ gem install date-performance
Fetching: date-performance-0.4.8.gem (100%)
Building native extensions.  This could take a while...
Successfully installed date-performance-0.4.8
1 gem installed
```

Let's see how Date from the standard library performs.

chp2/date_without_date_performance.rb
```
require 'date'
require 'benchmark'

GC.disable

memory_before = `ps -o rss= -p #{Process.pid}`.to_i/1024

time = Benchmark.realtime do
  100000.times do
    Date.new(2014,5,1)
  end
end

memory_after = `ps -o rss= -p #{Process.pid}`.to_i/1024

puts "time: #{time}, memory: #{"%d MB" % (memory_after - memory_before)}"
```

```
$ ruby date_without_date_performance.rb
time: 2.19644594192505, memory: 262 MB
```

We need 2.2 seconds to create 100,000 dates. Now let's compare this with Date::Performance.

chp2/date_with_date_performance.rb
```
require 'benchmark'
require 'rubygems'
require 'date/performance'

GC.disable

memory_before = `ps -o rss= -p #{Process.pid}`.to_i/1024

time = Benchmark.realtime do
  100000.times do
    Date.new(2014,5,1)
  end
end
```

```
memory_after = `ps -o rss= -p #{Process.pid}`.to_i/1024

puts "time: #{time}, memory: #{"%d MB" % (memory_after - memory_before)}"
```

```
$ ruby -I . date_with_date_performance.rb --no-gc
time: 0.294741868972778, memory: 84 MB
```

The same code written in C is almost eight times faster! And as a bonus it uses 175 MB less memory. Both are great improvements. That's why I advise that everybody who is stuck with a good old Ruby 1.8 should use the Date::Performance gem.

There are also gems that implement a specific task in C. The best example of this is markdown libraries. Some of them are written in C, some of them in Ruby. Here's the performance comparison made by Jashank Jeremy, one of the Jekyll blog engine contributors:

Gem	Language	Speed, posts/second
BlueCloth	C	60.7 ± 17.8
RedCarpet	C	56.1 ± 16.5
RDiscount	C	54.9 ± 16.6
Kramdown	Ruby	40.1 ± 8.4
Maruku	Ruby	17.1 ± 6.5

The slowest C implementation (RDiscount) is 1.4 times faster than the fastest Ruby one (Kramdown). The difference between the fastest and slowest is an impressive 3.5 times. As you can see, it makes total sense to search for gems that do the hard work in native code.

Takeaways

We saw in this chapter that there are only three things that you need to consider to make your Ruby code faster:

- Optimize memory by avoiding extra allocations and memory leaks.
- Write faster iterators that take both less time and memory.
- And finally, write less Ruby code by letting specialized tools do their job.

The beauty of these techniques is that you can apply them to any Ruby program to make it up to ten times faster. But the majority of the Ruby developers are writing Rails applications, so it's now time to dive deeper and apply our optimization techniques to Ruby on Rails.

## CHAPTER 3

Make Rails Faster

In principle, you already know how to make Rails faster: the same performance optimization strategies that we've discussed in the previous chapter will work for any Rails application. Use less memory, avoid heavy function calls in iterators, and write less Ruby and Rails. These are the big things that make Rails applications faster, and you'll learn how to apply them in this chapter.

But before we start, make sure you have at least a bare Rails application set up and running. All the examples you'll see in this chapter require a Rails 4.x application with a database connection. I'll also assume we are both using a PostgreSQL 9.x database. PostgreSQL is my preferred choice not only because it is one of the best-performing freely available databases. I choose it specifically because I will need a lot of random data for the examples, and that's easy to generate with the Postgres-specific generate_series function. That lets us start with an empty database and add schema and data in migrations as necessary.

So, take the Rails app (bare or your own), and let's optimize it.

Make ActiveRecord Faster

ActiveRecord is a wrapper around your data. By definition that should take memory, and oh indeed it does. It turns out the overhead is quite significant, in both the number of objects and in raw memory.

To see the overhead, let's create a database table with 10 string columns and fill it with 10,000 rows, each row containing 10 strings of 100 chars. (The code starts on the next page.)

```
chp3/app/db/migrate/20140722140429_large_tables.rb
class LargeTables < ActiveRecord::Migration
  def up
    create_table :things do |t|
      10.times do |i|
        t.string "col#{i}"
      end
    end

    execute <<-END
      insert into things(col0, col1, col2, col3, col4,
                          col5, col6, col7, col8, col9) (
        select
          rpad('x', 100, 'x'), rpad('x', 100, 'x'), rpad('x', 100, 'x'),
          rpad('x', 100, 'x'), rpad('x', 100, 'x'), rpad('x', 100, 'x'),
          rpad('x', 100, 'x'), rpad('x', 100, 'x'), rpad('x', 100, 'x'),
          rpad('x', 100, 'x')
        from generate_series(1, 10000)
      );
    END
  end
  def down
    drop_table :things
  end
end
```

This migration creates 10 million bytes of data (10,000 * 10 * 100), approximately 9.5 MB. A database is quite efficient at storing that. For example, my PostgreSQL installation uses just 11 MB:

```
$ psql app_development
app_development=# select pg_size_pretty(pg_relation_size('things'));
pg_size_pretty
----------------
11 MB
```

Let's see how memory-efficient ActiveRecord is. We'll need to create a Thing model:

```
chp3/app/app/models/thing.rb
class Thing < ActiveRecord::Base
end
```

And we'll need to adapt our wrapper.rb measurement helper from the previous chapter to Rails:

```
chp3/app/lib/measure.rb
class Measure

  def self.run(options = {gc: :enable})
    if options[:gc] == :disable
      GC.disable
    elsif options[:gc] == :enable
      # collect memory allocated during library loading
      # and our own code before the measurement
      GC.start
    end

    memory_before = `ps -o rss= -p #{Process.pid}`.to_i/1024
    gc_stat_before = GC.stat
    time = Benchmark.realtime do
      yield
    end
    gc_stat_after = GC.stat
    GC.start if options[:gc] == :enable
    memory_after = `ps -o rss= -p #{Process.pid}`.to_i/1024

    puts({
      RUBY_VERSION => {
        gc: options[:gc],
        time: time.round(2),
        gc_count: gc_stat_after[:count].to_i - gc_stat_before[:count].to_i,
        memory: "%d MB" % (memory_after - memory_before)
      }
    }.to_json)
  end

end
```

For this to work, add the lib directory to Rails' autoload_paths in config/application.rb.

```
chp3/app/config/application.rb
config.autoload_paths << Rails.root.join('lib')
```

Got that? Good. Now we can run our migration and measure the memory usage. Note that this needs to be done in production mode to make sure we do not include any of Rails development mode's side effects.

```
$ RAILS_ENV=production bundle exec rake db:create
$ RAILS_ENV=production bundle exec rake db:migrate
$ RAILS_ENV=production bundle exec rails console

2.2.0 :001 > Measure.run(gc: :disable) { Thing.all.load }
{"2.2.0":{"gc":"enable","time":0.32,"gc_count":1,"memory":"33 MB"}}
 => nil
```

ActiveRecord uses 3.5 times more memory than the size of the data. It also triggers one garbage collection during loading.

ActiveRecord is convenient, but the convenience that ActiveRecord affords comes at a steep price. I realize I'm not going to convince you to avoid ActiveRecord. But you do need to understand the consequences of using it. In 80% of cases, the speed of development is worth more than the cost in execution speed. In the remaining 20% of cases, you have other options. Let me show you them.

Load Only the Attributes You Need

Your first option is to load only the data you intend to use. Rails makes this very easy to do, like this:

```
$ RAILS_ENV=production bundle exec rails console
Loading production environment (Rails 4.1.4)

2.2.0 :001 > Measure.run { Thing.all.select([:id, :col1, :col5]).load }
{"2.2.0":{"gc":"enable","time":0.21,"gc_count":1,"memory":"7 MB"}}
 => nil
```

This uses 5 times less memory and runs 1.5 times faster than Thing.all.load. The more columns you have, the more it makes sense to add select into the query, especially if you join tables.

Preload Aggressively

Another best practice is preloading. Every time you query into a has_many or belongs_to relationship, preload.

For example, let's add a has_many relationship call to our Thing. We'll need to set up the migration and ActiveRecord model.

```
chp3/app/db/migrate/20140724142101_minions.rb
class Minions < ActiveRecord::Migration
  def up
    create_table :minions do |t|
      t.references :thing
      10.times do |i|
        t.string "mcol#{i}"
      end
    end

    execute <<-END
      insert into minions(thing_id,
                          mcol0, mcol1, mcol2, mcol3, mcol4,
                          mcol5, mcol6, mcol7, mcol8, mcol9) (
        select
          things.id,
```

```
        rpad('x', 100, 'x'), rpad('x', 100, 'x'), rpad('x', 100, 'x'),
        rpad('x', 100, 'x'), rpad('x', 100, 'x'), rpad('x', 100, 'x'),
        rpad('x', 100, 'x'), rpad('x', 100, 'x'), rpad('x', 100, 'x'),
        rpad('x', 100, 'x')
      from things, generate_series(1, 10)
    );
    END
  end
  def down
    drop_table :minions
  end
end
```

chp3/app/app/models/minion.rb
```
class Minion < ActiveRecord::Base
  belongs_to :thing
end
```

chp3/app/app/models/thing.rb
```
class Thing < ActiveRecord::Base
  has_many :minions
end
```

Run the migration with RAILS_ENV=production bundle exec rake db:migrate and you will get 10 Minions for each Thing in the database.

Iterating over that data without preloading is not such a good idea.

```
$ RAILS_ENV=production bundle exec rails console
Loading production environment (Rails 4.1.4)

2.2.0 :001 > Measure.run { Thing.all.each { |thing| thing.minions.load } }
{"2.2.0":{"gc":"enable","time":272.93,"gc_count":16,"memory":"478 MB"}}
=> nil
```

Good luck waiting for this one line of code to finish. It needs not only to load everything into memory, but also to execute 10,000 queries against the database to fetch the minions for each thing.

Preloading is the better way.

```
$ RAILS_ENV=production bundle exec rails console
Loading production environment (Rails 4.1.4)

2.2.0 :001 > Measure.run { Thing.all.includes(:minions).load }
{"2.2.0":{"gc":"enable","time":11.59,"gc_count":19,"memory":"518 MB"}}
=> nil
```

Depending on the Rails version, this might be slightly less memory efficient. But the code finishes 25 times faster because Rails performs only two database queries—one to load things, and another to load minions.

Combine Selective Attribute Loading and Preloading

Even better is to take my advice from the *Load Only the Attributes You Need* section and select only the columns we need. But there's a catch. Rails does not have a convenient way of selecting a subset of columns from the dependent model. For example, this will fail:

```
Thing.all.includes(:minions).select("col1", "minions.mcol4").load
```

It fails because includes(:minions) runs an additional query to fetch minions for the things it selected. And Rails is not smart enough to figure out which of the select columns belong to the Minions table.

If we queried from the side of the belongs_to association, we would use joins.

```
Minion.where(id: 1).joins(:thing).select("things.col1", "minions.mcol4")
```

From the has_many side joins will return duplicates of the same Thing object, 10 duplicates in our case. To combat that, we can use the PostgreSQL-specific array_agg feature that aggregates an array of columns from the joined table.

```
$ RAILS_ENV=production bundle exec rails console
Loading production environment (Rails 4.1.4)

2.2.0 :001 > query = "select id, col1, array_agg(mcol4) from things
2.2.0 :002">          inner join
2.2.0 :003">          (select thing_id, mcol4 from minions) minions
2.2.0 :004">          on (things.id = minions.thing_id)
2.2.0 :005">          group by id, col1"
 => "select id, col1, array_agg(mcol4) from things
     inner join
     (select thing_id, mcol4 from minions) minions
     on (things.id = minions.thing_id)
     group by id, col1"
2.2.0 :006 > Measure.run { Thing.find_by_sql(query) }
{"2.2.0":{"gc":"enable","time":0.62,"gc_count":1,"memory":"8 MB"}}
 => nil
```

Just look at the memory consumption: 8 MB instead of 518 MB from a full select with preloading. As a bonus, this runs 20 times faster.

Restricting the number of columns you select can save you seconds of execution time and hundreds of megabytes of memory.

Use the Each! Pattern for Rails with find_each and find_in_batches

It is expensive to instantiate a lot of ActiveRecord models. Rails developers knew that and added two functions to loop through large datasets in batches. Both find_each and find_in_batches will load by default 1,000 objects and return them to you—the first function, one by one; the latter, the whole batch at once. You can ask for smaller or larger batches with the :batch_size option.

find_each and find_in_batches will still have to load all the objects in memory. So how do they improve performance? The effect is the same as with the each! pattern from *Use the Each! Pattern*, on page 27. Once you're done with the batch, GC can collect it. Let's see how that works.

```
$ RAILS_ENV=production bundle exec rails console
Loading production environment (Rails 4.1.4)

2.2.0 :001 > ObjectSpace.each_object(Thing).count
 => 0
2.2.0 :002 > Thing.find_in_batches { |batch|
2.2.0 :003?>     GC.start
2.2.0 :004?>     puts ObjectSpace.each_object(Thing).count
2.2.0 :005?>   }
1000
2000
 … 6 lines elided
2000
2000
 => nil
2.2.0 :006 > GC.start
 => nil
2.2.0 :007 > ObjectSpace.each_object(Thing).count
 => 0
```

GC indeed collects objects from previous batches, so no more than two batches are in memory during the iteration. Compare this with the regular each iterator over the list of objects returned by Thing.all.

```
$ RAILS_ENV=production bundle exec rails console
Loading production environment (Rails 4.1.4)

2.2.0 :001 > ObjectSpace.each_object(Thing).count
 => 0
2.2.0 :002 > Thing.all.each_with_index { |thing, i|
2.2.0 :003?>     if i % 1000 == 0
2.2.0 :004?>       GC.start
2.2.0 :005?>       puts ObjectSpace.each_object(Thing).count
2.2.0 :006?>     end
2.2.0 :007?>   }; nil
10000
10000
 … 6 lines elided
10000
10000
 => nil
```

Here we keep 10,000 objects for the whole duration of the each loop. This increases both total memory consumption and GC time. It also increases the risk of running out of memory if the dataset is too big (remember, ActiveRecord needs 3.5 times more space to store your data).

Use ActiveRecord without Instantiating Models

If all you need is to run a database query or update a column in the table, consider using the following ActiveRecord functions that do not instantiate models.

- ActiveRecord::Base.connection.execute("select * from things")

  This function executes the query and returns its result unparsed.

- ActiveRecord::Base.connection.select_values("select col5 from things")

  Similar to the previous function, but returns an array of values only from the first column of the query result.

- Thing.all.pluck(:col1, :col5)

  Variation of the previous two functions. Returns an array of values that contains either the whole row or the columns you specified in the arguments to pluck.

- Thing.where("id < 10").update_all(col1: 'something')

  Updates columns in the table.

These not only save you memory, but also run faster because they neither instantiate models nor execute before/after filters. All they do is run plain SQL queries and, in some cases, return arrays as the result.

Make ActionView Faster

It's not unusual for template rendering to take longer than controller code. But you may think that you can't do much to speed it up. Most templates are just a collection of calls to rendering helper functions that you didn't write and can't really optimize—except when they're called in a loop.

Rendering is basically a string manipulation. As we already know, that takes both CPU time and memory. In a loop we multiply the effect of what is already slow. So every time you iterate over a large dataset in a template, see whether you can optimize it.

Rails template rendering has performance characteristics similar to Ruby iterators. It's fine to do just about anything, until you render partials in a loop. There are two reasons for that.

First, rendering comes at a cost. It takes time to initialize the view object, compute the execution context, and pass the required variables. So every partial that you render in a loop should be your first suspect for poor performance.

Second, the majority of Rails view helpers are iterator-unsafe. One call to link_to will not slow you down, but a thousand of them will.

These two potential performance problems are really the same as we have already discussed in *Avoid Iterators That Create Additional Objects*, on page 27 and *Watch for Iterator-Unsafe Ruby Standard Library Functions*, on page 29, just one level of abstraction higher, and they apply only to Rails. So let's discuss these problems in detail and see what we can optimize.

Render Partials in a Loop Faster

When asked to render a set of objects, your template code would probably look something like this:

```
<% objects.each do |object| %>
  <%= render partial: 'object', locals: { object: object } %>
<% end %>
```

There's nothing wrong with the code, except that it becomes slow on a large collection of objects. How slow? I measured the rendering of 10,000 empty partials in different versions of Rails and the results were not pleasant.

Rails 2.x	Rails 3.x	Rails 4.x
0.335 ± 0.006	1.355 ± 0.033	1.840 ± 0.045

Table 2—Time to render 10,000 partials
Measured with GC disabled, in seconds. Results scale linearly with the number of partials.

Although 10,000 objects is not a large dataset, just rendering the placeholders for them will set you back by 2 seconds with recent Rails. That's disturbing. Also disturbing is that rendering also gets much worse with each subsequent version of Rails. But before you fall into your memories of good old Rails 2.x times, let me point out that even 0.3 seconds for doing nothing is already too much.

Rails 3.0 and higher has a solution to this problem called render collection:

```
<%= render :partial => 'object', :collection => @objects %>
```

Or, in a shorter notation:

```
<%= render @objects %>
```

This inserts a partial for each member of the collection, automatically figuring out the partial name and passing the local variable.[1] That also performs 20 times faster.

Rails 3.x	Rails 4.x
0.066 ± 0.001	0.100 ± 0.005

Table 3—Time to render a collection of 10,000 objects
Empty partials. Measured with GC disabled, in seconds. Results scale linearly with the number of partials.

The reason rendering a collection is faster is that it initializes the template only once. Then it reuses the same template to render all objects from the collection. Rendering 10,000 partials in a loop will have to repeat the initialization 10,000 times.

How much work is it to initialize the template? I have profiled the rendering of 10,000 partials in Rails 4 to illustrate that. Let's look at the summary.

Operation	Percent of total execution time
Logging	45%
Finding and reading the template (from disk or cache)	21%
Setting up execution context (local variables, etc.)	9%
Template class instantiation	5%
Rendering	5%
Other work	15%

I'm sure we are both having our aha moment now. Actual rendering takes only 5% of the time. No wonder that if we skip initialization, we'll get two orders of magnitude speedup—exactly as in our measurements.

Let's see why logging takes 45% of the time. It turns out that with default config.log_level = :info in production mode Rails produces too much output.

```
INFO --: Started GET "/test" for 127.0.0.1 at 2014-08-13 10:21:40 -0500
INFO --: Processing by TestController#index as HTML
INFO --:   Rendered test/_object.html.erb (0.1ms)
«9998 more object.html.erb partial rendering notifications»
INFO --:   Rendered test/_object.html.erb (0.0ms)
INFO --:   Rendered test/_dummy.html.erb (1904.0ms)
INFO --:   Rendered test/index.html.erb within layouts/application (1945.4ms)
```

---

1.   http://guides.rubyonrails.org/layouts_and_rendering.html#rendering-collections

Joe asks:
But Rails Applications Rarely Need to Render 10,000 Partials, Do They?

Most likely not a lot of them render 10,000 partials. But 1,000 does not seem like an unreachable number. Let's do some math. Imagine you render 100 objects with a partial in a loop. Now imagine that partial calls 10 other partials. These numbers look legit. If you render a paginated table with 10 columns, you'll get a setup like this. How many render partial calls do we have? Already 1,000. How much time will we spend just inside the render partial function? About 200 ms according to my measurements. If we factor in the time for actually rendering useful content, we'll easily cross the 1-second response time mark. And that's already unacceptable for any web application.

```
INFO --: Completed 200 OK in 1952ms (Views: 1948.6ms | ActiveRecord: 0.0ms)
```

Chances are you won't want to silence your logs completely with config.log_level = :warn, but doing that would give you two times speedup.

config.log_level = :info	config.log_level = :warn
1.840 ± 0.045	0.830 ± 0.049

Table 4—Time to render a collection of 10,000 objects with different log levels
Rails 4. Empty partials. Measured with GC disabled, in seconds

That is still not as fast as render collection (0.1 s). Where do the remaining 0.7 seconds go? It turns out that Rails implements a logger using the Observer pattern. Partial rendering triggers a render_partial.action_view event. When that happens ActionSupport::LogSubscriber gets notified and, in turn, runs Logger to produce the output. This plumbing code takes about 0.2 seconds. Template initialization and execution context evaluation take the rest.

Render collection has none of that overhead, and it doesn't produce excessive log output, either. That makes it clearly superior to rendering partials in a loop.

There's no render collection in Rails 2.x. But if you're still using that version, try the template inliner plug-in.[2] It achieves the same effect by textually inserting partial code into the parent template before Rails compiles it.

---

2. https://github.com/acunote/template_inliner

This is what I wrote when I worked at Acunote,[3] the online project management system built with Ruby on Rails. There we rendered hundreds of tasks on the page, each task having 8–10 fields. For each field we had a separate partial for rendering, and there was no render collection in Rails 2.x. That's when the template inliner was born.

To use it, add the plug-in to your Rails application, and append inline: true to the render statement:

```
<% @objects.each do |object| %>
  <%= render partial: 'object', locals: { object: object }, inline: true %>
<% end %>
```

Rails never sees the render partial call, and as result, we get the same two orders of magnitude performance improvement.

Rails 2.x	Rails 2.x with template inliner
0.335 ± 0.006	0.003 ± 0.0001

Table 5—Time to render 10,000 partials inline

Measured with GC disabled, in seconds. Results scale linearly with the number of partials.

Avoid Iterator Unsafe Helpers and Functions

All rendering helpers are what I call iterator unsafe. They take both time and memory, so be careful when using them in a loop, especially with link_to, url_for, and img_tag.

I do not have any better advice than to be careful, for two reasons. First, you cannot avoid using these helpers (especially in newer Rails). Second, it's very hard to benchmark them. Helpers' performance depends on too many factors, making any synthetic benchmark useless. For example, link_to and url_for get slower when the complexity of your routing increases. And img_tag performs worse as you add more assets. In one application it's safe to render a thousand URLs in the loop, whereas in another it's not. So…be careful.

Takeaways

It takes the same techniques we learned in Chapter 2, *Fix Common Performance Problems*, on page 13 to make your Rails application faster:

- Optimize memory taken by ActiveRecord by aggressive preloading, selective attribute fetching, and data processing in batches.

---

3.   http://www.acunote.com/

- Replace explicit iterators in views with render collection, which takes both less time and memory.

- Let your database server do your data manipulation.

This and the two previous chapters contain all the advice I can give you to make your Ruby and Rails code faster. Go ahead, apply it, and reap your performance benefits. So why, you may ask, is this not the end of the book? Because any cookbook-style advice is only good for well-known situations. And it leaves you unprepared when performance degrades for an entirely different reason that I did not experience, or could not predict.

It's time to learn what to do if none of the advice works. When that happens, you'll need to profile your application, understand what can go wrong, optimize, measure, and make sure slowdown never happens again. In the next three chapters you'll learn how to do all that.

CHAPTER 4

Profile

All right, so you've learned the key performance optimization techniques and can apply them to your code. But what do you do when none of the techniques we've discussed work?

You profile.

Profiling is the only sure way to answer the question "What is slowing this code down?" Profiling can be hard and time consuming, but there's really no shortcut. If you can't optimize just by looking at the code or by taking an educated guess, you have to profile.

Once you know exactly what is slowing you down, fixing it becomes trivial. So now I'll teach you the arcane secrets of profiling, which will make finding out what's slow easier.

Let's start our exploration of profiling by breaking it down into its two basic parts. First, there's measuring memory or CPU usage and attributing this to specific places in the code, most often function calls. Second, there's interpreting the results to identify the slow parts of the code. These are two very different kinds of activities, and you need to think about them differently.

Measuring is a pure engineering task and is simple. You can do it by hand or use a profiler tool. I'll show you how to use the tools.

Interpreting measurements is more complicated, but the secret is to treat it as a craft, not as an engineering task. I've seen many brilliant software developers give up profiling precisely because they tried to profile as engineers. Your left brain will see profiling as cumbersome and unsatisfying. Involve your right brain, and instead you will find it intriguing and exciting.

Because profiling is a craft, I will teach it as that—in other words, by example. I'll show you how I profile my code using concrete examples, and I'll leave it for you to abstract the techniques that work for you. That'll be easy once you pick up the patterns in the examples. So turn on your right brain, and let's start.

Up to now I've kept telling you that you need to optimize memory first. But now we're going to reverse the order and look first at CPU profiling, and only then at memory. There are much better and more mature tools available for CPU optimization. Once you master them, you can apply the same approach to memory optimization, despite the inferior tools available for that task.

CPU profiling and optimization, then, is what you need to do to speed up algorithmically slow code.

For profiling we'll use the ruby-prof[1] tool. It will measure the execution time of your program and will break it down to individual functions that your program uses.

After you get the measurements from ruby-prof, you can visualize them either with the built-in ruby-prof printing tools or with KCachegrind.[2]

Both ruby-prof and KCachegrind are multiplatform and freely available. We'll go through examples of exactly how to use each of them in profiling your code, but first: the rules of CPU profiling.

There's just one. The first and the only rule of successful CPU profiling is: *turn off the garbage collector*. GC is unpredictable and hidden from any Ruby code, including the profiler itself. So instead of separating the GC time, the profiler will attribute it to the function that was running when GC kicked off. This will result in unhelpful advice like learning that the Fixnum::+ function takes 300 ms of execution time doing 2+2. To get meaningful results, always disable GC.

OK, let's pick up our first CPU profiling tool and get to work!

Measure with Ruby-Prof

ruby-prof is a Ruby gem that comes with both an API and a command-line tool. In most cases you'll probably want use the API to profile just that isolated part of the code that you suspect to be slow. But the command-line tool is what you want for profiling application startup, especially if you're interested in rubygems startup costs. In Rails applications you can get the complete request profile by inserting ruby-prof into the middleware stack.

---

1. https://github.com/ruby-prof/ruby-prof
2. http://kcachegrind.sourceforge.net/html/Home.html

1. ruby-prof API

In this example we'll use the ruby-prof API to profile a specific part of your code.

chp4/ruby_prof_example_api1.rb
```
require 'date'
require 'rubygems'
require 'ruby-prof'

GC.disable

RubyProf.start
Date.parse("2014-07-01")
result = RubyProf.stop

printer = RubyProf::FlatPrinter.new(result)
printer.print(File.open("ruby_prof_example_api1_profile.txt", "w+"))
```

Alternatively, you can pass a block to ruby-prof.

```
result = RubyProf.profile do
  Date.parse("2014-07-01")
end
```

The idea is to wrap the code, in our example the Date#parse call, between RubyProf.start and RubyProf.stop and then print the report.

There are several types of reports ruby-prof can print, but for now we'll use just one of them, called FlatPrinter, that shows the overall time spent in each function. The output is sorted by time, with functions that take the most time printed first, so you can easily see which functions are the CPU hogs.

Make sure you have the ruby-prof gem installed and run the program.

```
$ rbenv shell 2.1.5
$ gem install ruby-prof
$ ruby ruby_prof_example_api1.rb
```

Let's briefly take a look at the profile.

chp4/ruby_prof_example_api1_profile.txt
```
Thread ID: 70237499659060
Fiber ID: 70237507374720
Total: 0.001111
Sort by: self_time

%self     total     self      wait      child   calls  name
59.98     0.001     0.001     0.000     0.000     2   Regexp#match
28.96     0.001     0.000     0.000     0.001     1   <Class::Date>#parse
 4.72     0.001     0.000     0.000     0.001     1   Global#[No method]
```

3.81	0.000	0.000	0.000	0.000	1	String#gsub!
1.22	0.000	0.000	0.000	0.000	1	MatchData#begin
0.67	0.000	0.000	0.000	0.000	1	String#[]=
0.38	0.000	0.000	0.000	0.000	1	Fixnum#div
0.25	0.000	0.000	0.000	0.000	1	MatchData#end

```
* indicates recursively called methods
```

Our code spends more than 60% of its time matching the date I passed to the regular expression. Most of the remaining time is taken up by the Date#parse function itself, probably for Date instantiation.

Now let's see how to use the command-line tool.

2. ruby-prof Command-Line Tool

You don't have to add any instrumentation to the program itself in order to use the command-line tool. So the program can simply be this:

chp4/ruby_prof_example_command.rb
```
require 'date'

GC.disable
Date.parse("2014-07-01")
```

Run the ruby-prof command to profile it.

```
$ ruby-prof -p flat -m 1 -f ruby_prof_example_command_profile.txt\
    ruby_prof_example_command.rb
```

Here the -p option tells which printer to use to output the report (flat printer again in our case). And -m limits the outputs by suppressing all functions that took less than a specified percentage of time to execute. In this case I don't care about places where the code spends less than 1% of its time.

You should get a profile like this one:

chp4/ruby_prof_example_command_profile.txt
```
Thread ID: 69883126035220
Fiber ID: 69883132260680
Total: 0.002094
Sort by: self_time
```

%self	total	self	wait	child	calls	name
17.37	0.001	0.000	0.000	0.001	3	*Kernel#gem_original_requi
16.97	0.000	0.000	0.000	0.000	2	Regexp#match
10.85	0.001	0.000	0.000	0.000	1	<Class::Date>#parse
2.36	0.000	0.000	0.000	0.000	113	Module#method_added
1.83	0.000	0.000	0.000	0.000	6	IO#set_encoding
1.57	0.000	0.000	0.000	0.000	1	String#gsub!
1.23	0.000	0.000	0.000	0.000	6	MonitorMixin#mon_enter

```
1.16    0.002    0.000    0.000    0.002     2   Global#[No method]
1.12    0.000    0.000    0.000    0.000     3   Array#each
1.07    0.000    0.000    0.000    0.000    49   BasicObject#singleton_met
1.03    0.000    0.000    0.000    0.000     6   MonitorMixin#mon_exit
```

* indicates recursively called methods

With this profile you can see what took the most time during the whole program run. In this case it's Kernel#gem_original_require—the line that we didn't see when we profiled only date parsing. We can see the time spent in require 'date'. Other things like class and object initialization functions also appear in the profile. Unsurprisingly, our profile confirms that such a simple program spends more time on startup than on actual code execution.

Your profile may be a bit different, and sometimes GC#disable can appear at the top because it performs a lazy GC sweep before disabling. That may or may not take noticeable time depending on how many objects are currently marked for deletion in the memory heap. In case you're wondering what that GC sweep is that I'm talking about, take a peek at Chapter 10, *Tune Up the Garbage Collector*, on page 149. But don't think too much about GC#disable if you spot it here, as we have it in the source code only for profiling.

As I mentioned, a profile generated by the ruby-prof command-line tool is very useful if you're interested in the efficiency of application startup and gem loading. For other cases it adds too much data to the report, and you are much better off using the ruby-prof API.

3. Rails Middleware

The ruby-prof API works best if all you want is to profile a part of the Rails application—for example, controller action or template rendering. But to get insight into middleware, routing, and controller initialization, you need to insert ruby-prof as middleware.

To do that, add the ruby-prof gem into the Gemfile:

```
gem 'ruby-prof'
```

Also, insert the ruby-prof Rack adapter into the middleware stack in, for example, config/applilcation.rb:

```
config.middleware.use Rack::RubyProf, path: '/tmp/rails_profile'
```

The use call will insert the profiler into the bottom of the middleware stack. So the profile will include Rails initialization code, skipping the middleware. If you want to profile the middleware, insert the profiler before Rack::Runtime:

```
config.middleware.insert_before Rack::Runtime, Rack::RubyProf,
  path: '/tmp/rails_profile'
```

With Rack::RubyProf middleware loaded, you will get flat and HTML reports saved in the path you provide.

Don't forget to disable GC before Rack::RubyProf starts. The best way to do it is to write one more middleware and insert it before the profiler into the stack:

```ruby
class GCDisabler
  def initialize(app)
    @app = app
  end

  def call(env)
    GC.start
    GC.disable
    response = @app.call(env)
    GC.enable
    response
  end
end

# in config/application.rb
config.middleware.insert_before Rack::RubyProf, GCDisabler
```

Rails Profiling Best Practices

- Disable GC before profiling, as you should do for any Ruby code.

- Always profile in production mode. Development mode profiles are not useful because all you will see is class reloading and I/O operations made by noncached template initialization.

- Profile twice without restarting the application and discard the results of the first run to get the hot-start profile where everything is loaded and cached.

- If using Rails page or fragment caching, obtain two profiles: with and without caching.

Visualize with Ruby-Prof Printers

Ruby-prof can generate several types of human-readable reports. I find three of them to be the most useful: flat, call graph, and call stack reports. (You can see the full list in the ruby-prof documentation.)[3] Each serves a different

---

3. https://github.com/ruby-prof/ruby-prof

purpose. But we're learning by example here, and to show them to you, I'll need a more sophisticated example to profile.

```
chp4/app.rb
require 'date'
require 'rubygems'
require 'ruby-prof'

# This generates CSV like
# 1, John McTest, 1980-07-01
# 2, Peter McGregor, 1985-12-23
# 3, Sylvia McIntosh, 1989-06-13
def generate_test_data
  50000.times.map do |i|
    name = ["John", "Peter", "Sylvia"][rand(3)] + " " +
           ["McTest", "McGregor", "McIntosh"][rand(3)]
    [i, name, Time.at(rand * Time.now.to_i).strftime("%Y-%m-%d") ].join(',')
  end.join("\n")
end

def parse_data(data)
  data.split("\n").map! { |row| parse_row(row) }
end

def parse_row(row)
  row.split(",").map! { |col| parse_col(col) }
end

def parse_col(col)
  if col =~ /^\d+$/
    col.to_i
  elsif col =~ /^\d{4}-\d{2}-\d{2}$/
    Date.parse(col)
  else
    col
  end
end

def find_youngest(people)
  people.map! { |person| person[2] }.max
end

data = generate_test_data
GC.disable
result = RubyProf.profile do
  people = parse_data(data)
  find_youngest(people)
end

printer = RubyProf::FlatPrinter.new(result)
```

```
printer.print(File.open("app_flat_profile.txt", "w+"), min_percent: 3)

printer = RubyProf::GraphPrinter.new(result)
printer.print(File.open("app_graph_profile.txt", "w+"), min_percent: 3)

printer = RubyProf::CallStackPrinter.new(result)
printer.print(File.open("app_call_stack_profile.html", "w+"))
```

Our program generates random CSV with the list of people and their birth
dates, parses it, and finds the youngest person from that list. Here I parse
the CSV by hand to make the profile sophisticated, but still simple enough
to fully understand. At the end, I print the three reports I mentioned earlier.
I limit flat and graph reports to print-only functions that take more than 3%
of the total time.

The only external dependency of this example is the ruby-prof gem. I have a
Gemfile like the following and run the application with bundle exec ruby app.rb.

chp4/Gemfile
```
source 'https://rubygems.org'
gem 'ruby-prof', require: false
```

All clear? OK, let's run the app. It will generate three files: app_flat_profile.txt,
app_graph_profile.txt, and app_call_stack_profile.html. These correspond to the three
reports: flat, graph, and call stack. After you run the app, open these reports
in your editor or web browser, and let's see what useful information we can
extract from each of them.

Flat Report: Find Which Functions Are Slow

The flat profile shows the amount of time spent in each function. For our
example application, the flat profile looks like this:

chp4/app_flat_profile.txt
```
Thread ID: 70137029546800
Fiber ID: 70137039955760
Total: 1.882948
Sort by: self_time

  %self     total      self      wait     child     calls   name
  27.33     1.354     0.515     0.000     0.839    150000   Object#parse_col
  22.31     0.806     0.420     0.000     0.386     50000   <Class::Date>#parse
   8.59     0.162     0.162     0.000     0.000    100000   Regexp#match
   5.11     1.707     0.096     0.000     1.611     50000   Object#parse_row
   4.79     1.797     0.090     0.000     1.707     50002   *Array#map!
   4.66     0.088     0.088     0.000     0.000     50001   String#split
   4.46     0.084     0.084     0.000     0.000     50000   String#gsub!

* indicates recursively called methods
```

Let me first explain what the columns in the report mean.

%self The percentage of the time spent only in this function. See the definition of self.

total The total time spent in this function, including the execution time of functions that it calls.

self The time spent only in this function, excluding the execution time of functions that it calls.

wait The time spent waiting for other threads. This will always be zero for single-threaded apps. I'll sometimes omit this column from profiles included in this book to save some space.

child The time spent in functions that are called from the current function.

calls The total number of calls to this function.

The flat report is sorted by self time. So functions at the top of the report are the ones where our program spends most of the time.

For any given function, self time in the report is a sum of self times of all calls to that function, no matter where this call is in the code. For example, String#split is called once from the parse_data function and 50,000 times in the loop from parse_row. In the flat profile we see one line that reports all 50,001 String#split calls. All other metrics are also aggregated.

Also remember that self time doesn't include the time of nested function calls. For example, self time for Object#parse_col doesn't include the time of regular expression matching or date parsing. Despite being a simple-looking function with just an if-else statement, Object#parse_col still takes a considerable amount of time on its own. We'll discuss the reasons shortly, but for now just keep this in mind.

As we now know, the functions at the top are the slowest. So the first thing you should do is to optimize them. There's a chance this will make your code fast enough right away.

But often optimization doesn't end here. It's not enough to optimize the slowest functions by self time, for two reasons:

- The profiler may still report a large self time for a function even after you speed it up. For example, our top offender, Object#parse_col, does nothing on its own. All it really executes is an if-else statement. And it's still slow!

- The slowest function is either a library function, or simple enough already that you cannot further optimize it. In our example, Array#map! is the #3 slowest function. But it's a library routine that we can't really improve.

In both cases the slowness is caused by the number of function calls rather than by the function code itself. The obvious way to optimize in this situation is to reduce the number of function calls. For that you need to know where the function is called and how often. But our flat profile doesn't show that. It's time to look at another profile: the graph report.

Graph Report: Understand Which Parts of the Code Are Slow

The graph report is sorted by the total time spent in the function, including the time from functions that it calls. Let's look at the graph profile of our example application and figure out what it means.

```
chp4/app_graph_profile.txt
Thread ID: 70137029546800
Fiber ID: 70137039955760
Total Time: 1.8829480049999994
Sort by: total_time

  %total  %self     total    self   child        calls  Name
  --------------------------------------------------------------------
  100.00%  0.01%    1.883   0.000   1.883            1  Global#[No method]
                    1.777   0.000   1.777          1/1  Object#parse_data
                    0.106   0.000   0.106          1/1  Object#find_youngest
  --------------------------------------------------------------------
                    0.000   0.000   0.000  50000/50002  Object#parse_row
                    0.031   0.031   0.000      1/50002  Object#find_youngest
                    1.767   0.060   1.707      1/50002  Object#parse_data
   95.46%  4.79%    1.797   0.090   1.707        50002  *Array#map!
                    1.707   0.096   1.611  50000/50000  Object#parse_row
                    1.354   0.515   0.839 150000/150000 Object#parse_col
  --------------------------------------------------------------------
                    1.777   0.000   1.777          1/1  Global#[No method]
   94.39%  0.00%    1.777   0.000   1.777            1  Object#parse_data
                    1.767   0.060   1.707      1/50002  Array#map!
                    0.010   0.010   0.000      1/50001  String#split
  --------------------------------------------------------------------
                    1.707   0.096   1.611  50000/50000  Array#map!
   90.67%  5.11%    1.707   0.096   1.611        50000  Object#parse_row
                    0.077   0.077   0.000  50000/50001  String#split
                    0.000   0.000   0.000  50000/50002  Array#map!
  --------------------------------------------------------------------
                    1.354   0.515   0.839 150000/150000 Array#map!
   71.88% 27.33%    1.354   0.515   0.839       150000  Object#parse_col
                    0.806   0.420   0.386  50000/50000  <Class::Date>#parse
                    0.033   0.033   0.000  50000/50000  String#to_i
  --------------------------------------------------------------------
                    0.806   0.420   0.386  50000/50000  Object#parse_col
   42.79% 22.31%    0.806   0.420   0.386        50000  <Class::Date>#parse
                    0.162   0.162   0.000 100000/100000 Regexp#match
```

		0.084	0.084	0.000	50000/50000	String#gsub!
		0.046	0.046	0.000	50000/50000	String#[]=
		0.039	0.039	0.000	50000/50000	MatchData#begin
		0.031	0.031	0.000	50000/50000	Fixnum#div
		0.024	0.024	0.000	50000/50000	MatchData#end
		0.162	0.162	0.000	100000/100000	<Class::Date>#parse
8.59%	8.59%	0.162	0.162	0.000	100000	Regexp#match
		0.106	0.000	0.106	1/1	Global#[No method]
5.61%	0.00%	0.106	0.000	0.106	1	Object#find_youngest
		0.075	0.000	0.075	1/1	Enumerable#max
		0.031	0.031	0.000	1/50002	Array#map!
		0.010	0.010	0.000	1/50001	Object#parse_data
		0.077	0.077	0.000	50000/50001	Object#parse_row
4.66%	4.66%	0.088	0.088	0.000	50001	String#split
		0.084	0.084	0.000	50000/50000	<Class::Date>#parse
4.46%	4.46%	0.084	0.084	0.000	50000	String#gsub!
		0.075	0.000	0.075	1/1	Object#find_youngest
3.98%	0.00%	0.075	0.000	0.075	1	Enumerable#max
		0.075	0.035	0.040	1/1	Array#each
		0.075	0.035	0.040	1/1	Enumerable#max
3.98%	1.87%	0.075	0.035	0.040	1	Array#each
		0.040	0.040	0.000	49999/49999	Date#<=>

For this book I've generated the graph profile in the plain text format because it looks better on paper. But an HTML representation of the same report is easier to understand and more convenient to navigate because all function names are hyperlinks to their sections of the profile. To get the HTML report, replace the printer = RubyProf::GraphPrinter.new(result) line in our example with printer = RubyProf::GraphHtmlPrinter.new(result). It's a good idea to always use the HTML report for your own profiling needs.

The meaning of the columns is the same as for the flat report. I removed the wait column from graph reports included in this book so that they fit the page. We won't profile multithreaded applications, so the wait values will always be zero for us anyway.

Now let me guide you through this report. Each row contains the same function profiling data as in the flat profile, but with immediate function callers listed above and callees listed below.

The topmost function, called Global#nomethod, represents either part of code between RubyProf.start and RubyProf.end or a block passed to RubyProf.profile. It has no callers, so it comes first in its row. Below the Global#nomethod you see its two callees: Object#parse_data and Object#find_youngest. Each is called exactly one time. Hence the profile reports 1/1 calls, meaning that function is called one time from the global block and there is only one such function call in total.

The second row for Array#map! requires more effort to decipher. The function data line is now in the middle because there are both three callers above it and two callees below it. It may be confusing that the Array#map! data line is not the first in its row, but it's easy to tell it from callers and callees: it is the only line that has %total and %self values.

Total, self, and child times for the function data line have the same meaning as in the flat profile. These are, respectively, the total time that your program spends in the map iterator, the self time of the iterator function, and the time spent in the block that is passed to map and executed in a loop.

Let's look at Array#map! caller lines and try to make sense out of them.

The Calls column shows that we executed Array#map! 50,002 times: 50,000 of them from Object#parse_row, one from Object#find_youngest, and another one from Object#parse_data. A quick look at the application code confirms these numbers.

The timing columns for the caller lines have a slightly different meaning. For each caller line these show the total, self, and child times that Array#map! took while that caller executed it.

The timing for Object#parse_data and Object#find_youngest makes perfect sense. Parsing took an order of magnitude more time than selecting an element from the array in the find_youngest function.

But zeroes in total, self, and child times for Object#parse_row do not make any sense at the first sight. Row parsing is one of the slowest functions according to our flat profile, isn't it? The trick is that the Object#parse_data caller line already includes row parsing times because it calls parse_row in a loop. So the profiler in this case tries to prevent double counting and allocates the time only to the topmost function in the call stack. That happens to be Object#parse_data.

What useful information do we extract from this report? First, we get a high-level overview of where your program spends time. For example, our program spends almost 90% of its time iterating the data to parse CSV rows. Second, we can walk through the profile top-down to get an idea of which part of the code we should optimize. For example, we see that the slowest function by total time Array#map! calls Object#parse_row. That, in turn, calls String#split, which has a significant self time. So one way of optimizing would be to reduce the number of String#split calls or to replace them with something else.

But because of aggregation and double counting prevention, the graph report is still not good enough for top-down performance review. There's a better report for that: the call stack report.

Call Stack Report: Find Which Execution Path Is Slowest

This report really shows the call tree (not a stack as the name implies). Each node in the tree looks like this:

```
% of total time (% of caller time) Function [# of calls, # of calls total]
```

You get the percentage of this function's execution time (including its callees) relative to the total execution time, and the caller function's time. And you get the number of calls to this function within the current execution path and the total number of calls.

Let's see how the call stack profile looks for our example application.

chp4/app_call_stack_profile.txt
```
Call tree for application app.rb
Generated on 2014-10-02 08:53:27 -0500 with options {}
Threshold: [1.0] [Apply] [Expand All] [Collapse All] [Show Help]
Thread: 70137029546800, Fiber: 70137039955760 (100.00% ~ 1.8829480049999994)
    * [-] 100.00% (100.00%) Global#[No_method] [1 calls, 1 total]
        o [-] 94.39% (94.39%) Object#parse_data [1 calls, 1 total]
            # [-] 93.83% (99.41%) Array#map! [1 calls, 50002 total]
                # [-] 90.67% (96.63%) Object#parse_row [50000 calls,
                  50000 total]
                    # [-] 81.45% (89.84%) Array#map! [50000 calls,
                      50002 total]
                        # [-] 71.88% (88.25%) Object#parse_col
                          [150000 calls, 150000 total]
                            # [-] 42.79% (59.52%) <Class::
                              Date>#parse
                              [50000 calls, 50000 total]
                            # [ ] 1.76% (2.45%) String#to_i
                              [50000 calls, 50000 total]
                        # [ ] 4.10% (4.52%) String#split [50000 calls,
                          50001 total]
                # [ ] 0.56% (0.59%) String#split [1 calls, 50001 total]
        o [+] 5.61% (5.61%) Object#find_youngest [1 calls, 1 total]
            # [+] 3.98% (70.93%) Enumerable#max [1 calls, 1 total]
                # [+] 3.98% (99.98%) Array#each [1 calls, 1 total]
                    # [ ] 2.11% (52.96%) Date#<=> [49999 calls,
                      49999 total]
            # [ ] 1.63% (29.06%) Array#map! [1 calls, 50002 total]
```

You can read it top-down exactly as you would read the Ruby code. Our code snippet that we profile calls the parse_data and find_youngest functions. parse_data calls parse_row in a loop. That, in turn, calls parse_col in another loop.

What I like about this type of profile is that the total time percentages are not aggregated between code branches. Here's what I mean: Both flat and graph reports have only one line for Array#map! in the profile, but it's actually called from three different places in the code. In contrast, this is exactly what you see in the call stack profile. In our example profile you clearly see that a map from find_youngest takes less than 2% of the execution time, whereas the map that parses columns accounts for about 90% of the total time.

The percentage of caller time is useful to see which branch of code is slower. For example, in the find_youngest branch, two-thirds of the time is spent finding the maximum element in the array and only one-third of the time preparing that array.

The call stack profile is definitely easier to understand than the flat or graph profiles. I would even call it intuitive. But such a report works best for small chunks of code. Profiling a large codebase will give you a huge report, less suitable for optimization than for learning how the unfamiliar code works.

That's why my recommendation is to start with aggregated flat and graph reports and refer to the call stack report only when the data from those two is unclear.

And even when you can't seem to make sense out of the aggregated reports, a proper visualization tool can help you more than the call stack report will. Let me show you one such tool.

Visualize with KCachegrind (QCachegrind)

Ruby-prof can generate profiles in so-called *callgrind* format. This is the format used by the Valgrind profiler used in the C and C++ world. With the *CallTree-Printer*, you can obtain the callgrind-formatted profile and reuse some of the best visualization tools developed by C/C++ programmers.

KCachegrind[4] is, in my opinion, the best such tool. It comes as a part of all major Linux distributions. Its version for Mac OS and Windows is called QCachegrind. On Mac you can install it via MacPorts or Homebrew. On Windows you can use precompiled packages.[5]

---

4.   http://kcachegrind.sourceforge.net/html/Home.html

5.   http://sourceforge.net/projects/qcachegrindwin/

If you want to follow along, install it now, if necessary. And then let's take our example application and generate the callgrind output. Add this code snippet to the end of app.rb:

```
chp4/app.rb
printer = RubyProf::CallTreePrinter.new(result)
printer.print(File.open("callgrind.out.app", "w+"))
```

This will generate a file called callgrind.out.app. Callgrind has a strange naming convention where the file takes a callgrind.out prefix instead of an extension (suffix). After the prefix comes the name of the executable file, app in our case.

The file format is textual, but it's optimized for machine reading. So let's open KCachegrind or QCachegrind and see how it looks and what visualizations we have.

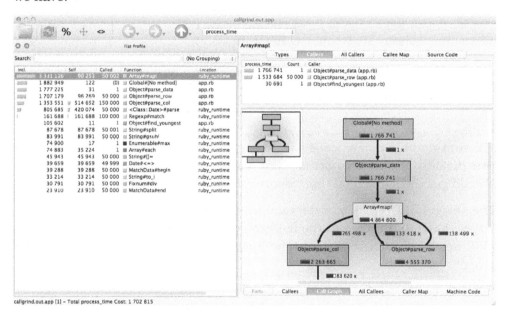

Flat Profile and Callers List

The list at the left looks like the same flat profile that ruby-prof's flat printer generates, except that it is sorted by Incl. time (total time in ruby-prof's parlance) by default. Clicking on the column will change the sorting.

While the profile looks the same as ruby-prof's flat profile, in reality it's not. Timings are different. So let's take a closer look at this profile and try to understand why and how it differs.

			Flat Profile		
Search:				(No Grouping)	

Incl.	Self	Called	Function	Location
3 331 116	90 253	50 002	Array#map!	ruby_runtime
1 882 949	122	(0)	Global#[No method]	app.rb
1 777 225	31	1	Object#parse_data	app.rb
1 707 179	96 269	50 000	Object#parse_row	app.rb
1 353 551	514 652	150 000	Object#parse_col	app.rb
805 685	420 074	50 000	<Class::Date>#parse	ruby_runtime
161 688	161 688	100 000	Regexp#match	ruby_runtime
105 602	11	1	Object#find_youngest	app.rb
87 678	87 678	50 001	String#split	ruby_runtime
83 991	83 991	50 000	String#gsub!	ruby_runtime
74 900	17	1	Enumerable#max	ruby_runtime
74 883	35 224	1	Array#each	ruby_runtime
45 943	45 943	50 000	String#[]=	ruby_runtime
39 659	39 659	49 999	Date#<=>	ruby_runtime
39 288	39 288	50 000	MatchData#begin	ruby_runtime
33 214	33 214	50 000	String#to_i	ruby_runtime
30 791	30 791	50 000	Fixnum#div	ruby_runtime
23 910	23 910	50 000	MatchData#end	ruby_runtime

The first notable difference is that Incl. and Self times are in microseconds. If you divide the Global#[No method] time you see in KCachegrind by 10^6, you should get the same total time reported by flat and graph profiles.

The second difference is in the total time for the Array#map function. It's way larger than what we see in the flat profile. Confusingly, it is also larger than total app execution time! Self time appears to be the same, though. What gives?

Remember that when we looked at the graph profile, we discussed the double counting prevention that ruby-prof has. KCachegrind does no such thing. This is why the Incl. time for Array#map includes its time when called from Object#find_youngest, Object#parse_data, *and* Object#parse_col. The last is called from parse_data and should have not been counted.

This way, total time for Array#map is a sum of its times inside all caller functions. You can clearly see this in KCachegrind in the second list view on the right, in the Callers tab.

Array#map!

Types	Callers	All Callers	Callee Map	Source Code

process_time	Count	Caller
1 766 741	1	Object#parse_data (app.rb)
1 533 684	50 000	Object#parse_row (app.rb)
30 691	1	Object#find_youngest (app.rb)

If you add the process_time numbers, you'll get the same Incl. time that you see in the flat profile view.

Except for the differences we have just seen, all other data should be the same as in ruby-prof's flat profile.

Callee and Caller Maps

When all you want is to quickly see where the whole application or any given function spends its time, look at the *callee map*. It shows functions as nested blocks. The area of each block is proportional to its Incl. time.

You can get the callee map for any function. For example, this is the map for Global#[No method]. That is the name for the whole code part that we profile.

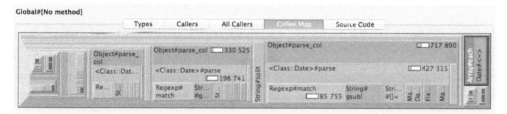

As expected, we see Object#parse_col, Date#parse, and Regexp#match taking most of the space. Object#parse_col has both significant self and total times. Its self time is visible in this report as the area not occupied by nested functions.

This view makes it easy to get an idea, graphically, of what takes time without digging through the numbers from the flat profile. But beware of the two shortcomings.

First, it tends to visualize nested calls as recursive. In reality Array#map calls Object#parse_row in a loop, which, in turn, calls Array#map again to parse columns. There's no recursion here—just two nested loops. What we see in the chart is instead the recursive call from Array#map to Object#parse_row, and recursively to Array#map and, again, Object#parse_row. KCachegrind is not smart enough to understand that the map that iterates over rows is different from the map that iterates over columns, and confuses them with the recursion.

Second, it double counts. Select the Array#map line in the Flat Profile view at the left and look at its callee map.

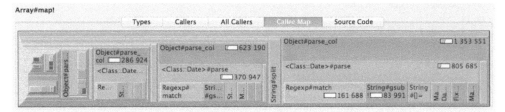

See how the largest box for Object#parse_col already reports 100% of its total time. And subsequent calls in the loop show more and more Object#parse_col boxes. Remember, we saw Array#map Incl. time double counting in the previous section. Column parsing is done within that map iterator, so its time is miscalculated as well, and distributed among the Array#map boxes in the chart.

Once you're aware of the potential miscalculations, the Callee Map view can be very useful in the first stages of the optimization. Caller Map at the bottom of the KCachegrind window is the similar view that shows an area chart of the function's callers. You should exercise similar caution when interpreting its results. Incorrect nesting and double counting are possible.

Source Code

The Callgrind format lets profilers store full path and line numbers of profiled functions. Ruby-prof does that for Ruby code so you can look inside the source with KCachegrind. For example, this is how Global#nomethod's source code view looks:

```
Global#[No method]
        Types    Callers    All Callers    Callee Map    Source Code
#    process_time    Source ('/Users/gremlin/adrpo/Book/code/chp4/app.rb')
39                   data = generate_test_data
40                   GC.disable
41                   result = RubyProf.profile do
42            122    people = parse_data(data)
     1 777 225       1 call(s) to 'Object#parse_data' (app.rb)
43                   find_youngest(people)
        105 602      1 call(s) to 'Object#find_youngest' (app.rb)
44                   end
45
46                   printer = RubyProf::FlatPrinter.new(result)
```

Lines that we are not profiling are grayed out. Each line for which ruby-prof has performance data is annotated with Incl. time. Double-clicking on the annotation line lets you dive into the callee function.

Unfortunately, KCachegrind doesn't show you the source of Ruby C standard library functions. Ruby-prof knows neither where to find Ruby sources nor how to find the function implementation there. Despite that, browsing the profile by reviewing the actual code can reveal information that you wouldn't otherwise get. For example, you can spot code that does nothing, or debug output.

Call Graph

The last view I'm going to talk about here is the call graph, and it's the most useful one in KCachegrind. It represents the same information that we have already seen in ruby-prof's graph report, but as an actual graph rendered by the dot tool from the GraphViz package.

KCachegrind can draw the call graph for any function that you select in the Flat Profile view. Choose Global#nomethod to get the graph for the entire code that you profile. This is how it looks for our example program:

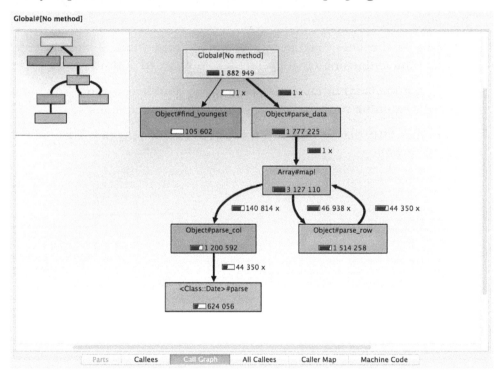

Here you can see the distribution of execution time between functions even more easily than with default ruby-prof's graph report. Also, all boxes on the chart are clickable, so you can dive in and see the call graph for any given function.

Double counting is a concern here, similar to other visualizations. Array#map has extra Incl. time once again.

Your intuition may suggest that you'll get the most value from the call graph by reading it from top to bottom and focusing on the branch where your program spends the most time. But double counting invalidates this approach.

The right way to look at a call graph is a bottom-up, breadth-first search and optimization. First, you look at the graph leaves and optimize them. Then you move up and try to optimize the next level of nodes, and so on. In the next chapter I'll show you how we can optimize our example application using this approach.

Takeaways

Let's review what you just learned about profiling:

- Use ruby-prof for profiling. Get better profile visualization with KCachegrind/QCachegrind.

- Profiling is the only reliable way to understand what is slow in your application. Unfortunately it doesn't tell you how to optimize.

- Profiling and visualization tools are prone to double counting. You must carefully examine your profile to draw the right conclusions.

- Remember little details that can make your profiles invalid. Turn off GC for CPU profiling.

## CHAPTER 5

Learn to Optimize with the Profiler

The profiler gives you plenty of information with different reports and visualizations. To optimize, your job is to take all that information, make an educated guess on what might be slow, optimize that, reprofile, and see whether your guess was correct.

Profiling is always guesswork. There's nothing deterministic except for the general routine of profile, guess, optimize, then profile again and repeat. Do not expect an ultimate profiler report that will magically tell you what's slow. Every report or visualization is looking into your app's performance from one specific angle. You might be able to see the problem from that angle, but most often you will not. Worse, miscounting and double counting obstruct the data even more.

So how do you profile then? Remember I told you that profiling is a craft. I can start you off by profiling our example app that we wrote in the previous section, but then you'll have to go out in the wild and profile for yourself. With time, you'll master this craft, and you'll be able to see the real sources of performance problems. So let's jump right in and optimize our example application.

Optimize but Don't Break

We'll start our profiling session by writing a test and a benchmark. Why? Because optimization means making changes to the code, most often to its core part. Sometimes, optimization requires complex architectural changes. And we should be able to make substantial changes without fearing we'll break things. This is why we need the test. We'll use the test to make sure we didn't break anything during optimization. Benchmarking is important because, as you'll see later, the speedup in the profiler won't always translate to the same improvement in the real world. So we need to measure our code's performance before and after optimization to ensure that things got faster.

We'll embed the test directly into the application and add the --test command-line option to run the test suite. Without the option, the program will run the profiler as before.

With --benchmark option we'll run our code outside the profiler and measure and print the execution time.

```ruby
chp4/app.rb
# «...»
if ARGV[0] == "--test"

  ARGV.clear
  require 'minitest/autorun'

  class AppTest < MiniTest::Unit::TestCase

    def setup
      @parsed_data = parse_data(generate_test_data)
    end

    def test_parsing
      assert_equal @parsed_data.length, 50000
      assert @parsed_data.all? do |row|
        row.length == 3 && row[0].class == Fixnum && row[2].class == Date
      end
    end

    def test_find_youngest
      youngest = find_youngest(@parsed_data)
      assert @parsed_data.all? { |row| youngest >= row }
    end

  end

  exit(0)
elsif ARGV[0] == "--benchmark"

  require 'benchmark'

  data = generate_test_data
  result = Benchmark.realtime do
    people = parse_data(data)
    find_youngest(people)
  end
  puts "%5.3f" % result

  exit(0)
```

```
else
  data = generate_test_data
  GC.disable
  result = RubyProf.profile do
    people = parse_data(data)
    find_youngest(people)
  end
end
# «...»
```

The first test_parsing test checks that we got the right number of columns and rows after parsing and that the data types were recognized correctly. The second test_youngest checks that we indeed found the latest birth date from the parsed data.

Let's run the test and make sure it passes.

```
$ bundle exec ruby app.rb --test
# Running tests:

..
Finished tests in 5.427569s, 0.3685 tests/s, 0.5527 assertions/s.
2 tests, 3 assertions, 0 failures, 0 errors, 0 skips
```

Let's also benchmark the application before optimization.

```
$ bundle exec ruby app.rb --benchmark
0.937
```

Pick Low-Hanging Fruit

Finally, it's time to optimize. We'll start by looking at the flat profile in KCachegrind and sort it by Self time, as shown in the figure on page 76.

Object#parse_col comes first, taking more than half a second of execution time. The function itself is not that slow, but we call it 150,000 times. Also, it calls two slow functions: <Class::Date>#parse and Regexp#match.

We should definitely concentrate our optimization on this group of three functions. Why is column parsing so slow? It's not because it takes too much time to parse one row. We do that in about 3 microseconds, but repeat that 150,000 times (50,000 rows multiplied by 3 columns). Can we reduce the number of repetitions? Not unless we change the way we parse the data or the amount of data itself.

Before we make any big architectural changes to the program, let's search for the low-hanging fruit in the parse_col function itself.

Incl.		Self		Called	Function	Location
	1 353 551	514 652		150 000	Object#parse_col	app.rb
	805 685	420 074		50 000	\<Class::Date>#parse	ruby_runtime
	161 688	161 688		100 000	Regexp#match	ruby_runtime
	1 707 179	96 269		50 000	Object#parse_row	app.rb
	3 331 116	90 253		50 002	Array#map!	ruby_runtime
	87 678	87 678		50 001	String#split	ruby_runtime
	83 991	83 991		50 000	String#gsub!	ruby_runtime
	45 943	45 943		50 000	String#[]=	ruby_runtime
	39 659	39 659		49 999	Date#<=>	ruby_runtime
	39 288	39 288		50 000	MatchData#begin	ruby_runtime
	74 883	35 224		1	Array#each	ruby_runtime
	33 214	33 214		50 000	String#to_i	ruby_runtime
	30 791	30 791		50 000	Fixnum#div	ruby_runtime
	23 910	23 910		50 000	MatchData#end	ruby_runtime
	1 882 949	122		(0)	Global#[No method]	app.rb
	1 777 225	31		1	Object#parse_data	app.rb
	74 900	17		1	Enumerable#max	ruby_runtime
	105 602	11		1	Object#find_youngest	app.rb

```
chp4/app.rb
def parse_col(col)
  if col =~ /^\d+$/
    col.to_i
  elsif col =~ /^\d{4}-\d{2}-\d{2}$/
    Date.parse(col)
  else
    col
  end
end
```

Inside we see the Date#parse that's responsible for about 800 ms on its own. Yes, we can expect that parsing dates is slow. But let's see what it's doing internally. Let's select its Date#parse in the flat profile and look at the call graph in the bottom-right view, shown in the image on page 77.

OK, it uses regular expressions to extract the year, month and date numbers. But wait, we already do that ourselves in the elsif statement. Date#parse just repeats the same thing. So why don't we use results of our own parsing and create a Date instance ourselves? Well, let's try that.

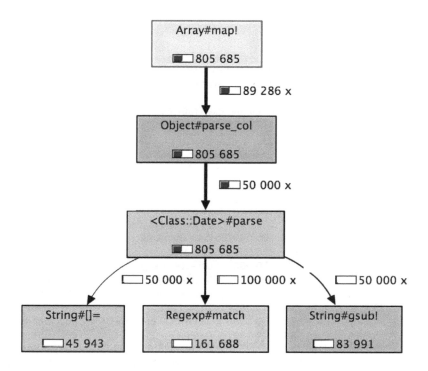

chp5/app_optimized1.rb
```ruby
def parse_col(col)
  if col =~ /^\d+$/
    col.to_i
  elsif match = /^(\d{4})-(\d{2})-(\d{2})$/.match(col)
    Date.new(match[1].to_i, match[2].to_i, match[3].to_i)
  else
    col
  end
end
```

In addition to changing parsing to object creation, we had to make two other changes. First, the regular expression now has three groups to capture: year, month, and day. Second, we converted the captured results to integers because the Date constructor doesn't accept string arguments.

We'll need to compare profiles before and after optimization, so we'll save the new profile to a different file.

chp5/app_optimized1.rb
```ruby
printer = RubyProf::CallTreePrinter.new(result)
printer.print(File.open("callgrind.out.app_optimized1", "w+"))
```

Before reprofiling, we run the tests to make sure we didn't break anything while optimizing.

```
$ bundle exec ruby app.rb --test
# Running tests:

..
Finished tests in 4.115975s, 0.4859 tests/s, 0.7289 assertions/s.
2 tests, 3 assertions, 0 failures, 0 errors, 0 skips
```

Let's run the application with bundle exec ruby app.rb, go to KCachegrind, open the new profile, and compare it to the original one.

Incl.	Self	Called	Function	Location
971 733	572 419	150 000	Object#parse_col	app_optimized1.rb
150 093	150 093	100 000	Regexp#match	ruby_runtime
112 405	112 405	200 000	String#to_i	ruby_runtime
1 311 665	93 891	50 000	Object#parse_row	app_optimized1.rb
92 180	92 180	150 000	MatchData#[]	ruby_runtime
2 541 216	81 000	50 002	Array#map!	ruby_runtime
79 396	79 396	50 001	String#split	ruby_runtime
44 636	44 636	50 000	<Class::Date>#new	ruby_runtime
43 988	43 988	49 999	Date#<=>	ruby_runtime
80 780	36 792	1	Array#each	ruby_runtime
1 483 947	261	(0)	Global#[No method]	app_optimized1.rb
1 375 723	35	1	Object#parse_data	app_optimized1.rb
80 803	23	1	Enumerable#max	ruby_runtime
107 963	12	1	Object#find_youngest	app_optimized1.rb

Search: | (No Grouping)

Hey, we actually optimized something! Look at the Incl. time for Global#[No method]. We reduced it by about 500 ms—that's a 20% speedup. Yes, we've added about 100 ms for string-to-integer conversion, and we do take additional time to extract groups out of matched strings. But we optimized the 800 ms that date parsing took. So we came out net positive despite additional work our program has to do.

What's next? Let's look at the flat profile one more time. Object#parse_col is still slow for no obvious reason. Remember, it's just an if/else statement that doesn't do anything on its own. So we'll skip it and look at what's next: regexp matching and string-to-integer conversion. We can't really get rid of the latter because it's a part of our new manual date parsing code. So let's look what can we do with the former. Go back again to the source.

```
chp5/app_optimized1.rb
def parse_col(col)
  if col =~ /^\d+$/
    col.to_i
  elsif match = /^(\d{4})-(\d{2})-(\d{2})$/.match(col)
```

```
      Date.new(match[1].to_i, match[2].to_i, match[3].to_i)
    else
      col
    end
end
```

Let's take a wild guess. What if we merge the two regexp matches in the if and elsif branches like this, retest, and reprofile?

chp5/app_optimized2.rb
```
def parse_col(col)
  if match = /^(\d+)$|^(\d{4})-(\d{2})-(\d{2})$/.match(col)
    if match[1]
      match[1].to_i
    else
      Date.new(match[2].to_i, match[3].to_i, match[4].to_i)
    end
  else
    col
  end
end
```

Incl.	Self	Called	Function	Location
1 174 580	501 569	150 000	Object#parse_col	app_optimized2.rb
316 979	316 979	150 000	Regexp#match	ruby_runtime
190 610	190 610	300 000	MatchData#[]	ruby_runtime
116 590	116 590	200 000	String#to_i	ruby_runtime
1 534 755	96 315	50 000	Object#parse_row	app_optimized2.rb
2 986 222	86 229	50 002	Array#map!	ruby_runtime
83 264	83 264	50 001	String#split	ruby_runtime
48 832	48 832	50 000	<Class::Date>#new	ruby_runtime
35 450	35 450	49 999	Date#<=>	ruby_runtime
62 863	27 412	1	Array#each	ruby_runtime
1 694 157	189	(0)	Global#[No method]	app_optimized2.rb
1 601 424	31	1	Object#parse_data	app_optimized2.rb
62 878	16	1	Enumerable#max	ruby_runtime
92 544	13	1	Object#find_youngest	app_optimized2.rb

But this time there's no improvement. We even lost about 200 ms if you compare Incl. time for Global#[No method] between this and previous optimization attempts. Why? The flat profile can tell us. Look how increased complexity of the regular expression matcher negated any potential benefits by taking twice as much time.

So this optimization didn't work. What lesson have we just learned? Always complete the profile–optimize–profile cycle. Your "optimization" might not be an optimization at all. You never know unless you reprofile.

What else can we optimize? Let's tackle an issue of large self time of Object#parse_col. It takes 27% of total execution time. That's too much self time for a function that's just an if-else statement that calls another function. What's the deal?

Since there's no code other than function calls, then it must be a function call itself that takes this much time. Ruby is an interpreted language, and there's a cost to any function call because of that.

Let's look again at the code and estimate how many functions Object#parse_col calls.

```
chp5/app_optimized3.rb
    def parse_col(col)
①     if col =~ /^\d+$/
②       col.to_i
③     elsif match = /^(\d{4})-(\d{2})-(\d{2})$/.match(col)
④       Date.new(match[1].to_i, match[2].to_i, match[3].to_i)
      else
        col
      end
⑤   end
```

❶ Two calls: Regexp#initialize and String#=~. These are part of the if condition and are executed every time we call Object#parse_col.

❷ One call to String#to_i. Executed only in one-third of the cases because we have three columns to parse in our example data and only one of the columns is a number.

❸ Again two calls, to Regexp#initialize and Regexp#match. These are executed in two-thirds of the cases.

❹ Date constructor call. We have one date column out of three, hence it's executed only in one-third of the cases.

❺ While this is not exactly a function call, there's some work that Ruby does to return the value from a function.

In total we have an average of $2 + \frac{1}{3} + \frac{2}{3} + \frac{1}{3} + \frac{1}{3} = 3\frac{2}{3}$ function calls and one value returned from each Object#parse_col invocation.

To test our theory we'll add a fake column parsing function that will call another dummy function $3\frac{2}{3}$ times on average. We'll make 150,000 calls to our fake function, the same number as the real one gets, and compare their self times.

```
chp5/app_optimized3.rb
def dummy
end

def fake_parse_col
  dummy; dummy;
  dummy if rand < 2/3.0
end
# «...»
data = generate_test_data
GC.disable
result = RubyProf.profile do
  people = parse_data(data)
  find_youngest(people)
  150000.times { fake_parse_col }
end

printer = RubyProf::CallTreePrinter.new(result)
printer.print(File.open("callgrind.out.app_optimized3", "w+"))
```

Our fake column parsing function makes three function calls at all times: two of them are to dummy and one of them to rand. In two-thirds of the cases there's one more dummy invocation. That roughly accounts for $3\frac{2}{3}$ function calls per one fake_parse_col.

Let's look at the flat profile in KCachegrind.

Incl.		Self	Called	Function	Location
▦	806 080	476 142	150 000	Object#parse_col	app_optimized3.rb
▦	646 919	414 567	150 000	Object#fake_parse_col	app_optimized3.rb

It turns out our theory is correct. Look how similar the self times are for Object#parse_col and Object#fake_parse_col. Does this mean there's a large cost to a function call in Ruby? Not necessarily. Remember, we run our code in the profiler that does extra work (usually measurements) per each function call.

What part of that cost is the profiler upkeep? It's easy to find out—we'll just run the same code from the Ruby console without any profiler and use Benchmark.realtime for measurements.

```
> irb
irb(main):001:0> def dummy
irb(main):002:1> end
```

```
=> :dummy
irb(main):003:0> def fake_parse_col
irb(main):004:1>    dummy; dummy;
irb(main):005:1*    dummy if rand < 2/3.0
irb(main):006:1> end
=> :fake_parse_col
irb(main):007:0> require 'benchmark'
=> true
irb(main):008:0> Benchmark.realtime { 150000.times { fake_parse_col } }
=> 0.049100519
```

That's approximately 10 times faster than in the profiler. What's our conclusion? Profiler adds up to 10 times to the Ruby function call cost, so we don't need to optimize the functions with large self times. Without the profiler they won't cause a performance problem.

Take a Step Back

Looking at the profile again, we think we collected all the low-hanging fruit there. Row parsing is still slow, though. The first five rows in the flat profile are for functions that do that parsing. In short, we optimized individual functions, but the whole thing is still slow.

In such cases the next step in optimization is to look at the code at a higher abstraction level. In our case we'll need to reexamine what the parsing code does. The first thing we note is that our code doesn't take advantage of the fact that column order is predefined. The first column is always a number, the second a name, and the third a date. So instead of determining the column type in the if/else statement, we can just go ahead and parse it. The date format is also predefined—there's no need to parse it with a regular expression. Instead we can extract date parts by their position. So, let's try out these ideas.

```
chp5/app_optimized4.rb
def parse_row(row)
  col1, col2, col3 = row.split(",")
  [
      col1.to_i,
      col2,
      Date.new(col3[0,4].to_i, col3[5,2].to_i, col3[8,2].to_i)
  ]
end
```

Tests pass, and the new profile looks like this:

Incl.	Self	Called	Function	Location
663 024	175	(0)	Global#[No method]	app_optimized4.rb
600 632	80 429	2	Array#map!	ruby_runtime
582 935	30	1	Object#parse_data	app_optimized4.rb
520 203	237 009	50 000	Object#parse_row	app_optimized4.rb
102 922	102 922	200 000	String#to_i	ruby_runtime
80 730	80 730	150 000	String#[]	ruby_runtime
79 914	13	1	Object#find_youngest	app_optimized4.rb
69 083	69 083	50 001	String#split	ruby_runtime
52 690	15	1	Enumerable#max	ruby_runtime
52 675	25 755	1	Array#each	ruby_runtime
39 942	39 942	50 000	<Class::Date>#new	ruby_runtime
26 920	26 920	49 999	Date#<=>	ruby_runtime

Ta-da! This code is more than two times faster! With a simple change, we eliminated regular expressions altogether. All that's left from parsing are String#to_i and String#[]. Together they take less than 30% of execution time. That's not bad.

Now our program is almost three times faster than it originally was. That's already impressive, and now it's time to decide whether it's worth it to optimize further. That's the decision you'll need to make every time you do significant optimization. I think three times is good enough, and the best is the enemy of the good. So let's stop here.

Does our optimization session ends with the decision to stop profiling? Not at all. Here comes the most important part. We'll benchmark the program without the profiler and check whether we'll see the same three times speedup. Here's the new number from Benchmark.realtime:

```
$ bundle exec ruby app_optimized4.rb --benchmark
0.201
```

Before optimization, the execution time was 0.937 seconds. After optimization, it's just 0.201 seconds. That's 4.7 times faster! The real-world effect is even better than the one we saw in the profiler.

Takeaways

Here's what you learned during this profiling session:

- Optimization with the profiler is a craft, not engineering.

  You must look at the data, make your best guess at what's slow, change the code, reprofile, and see whether your optimization worked. Rinse and repeat. The best way to learn this craft is by doing it. The more you profile, the better you understand the results you get, and the better optimization guesses you make.

- Write tests before profiling.

  You'll change the code a lot during profiling. Tests are your only way to ensure the program still does what it's supposed to do.

- The profiler will tell you what to optimize or where to concentrate your optimization effort.

  In our profiling session example, the profiler focused our attention on column parsing. First, we optimized date parsing. Second, we got rid of regular expressions. Once we did that, it turned out there wasn't much else to optimize.

- Optimize details, but never forget about the big picture.

  We had to go one layer of abstraction up to make our best optimization. It's worth rethinking what the code does. When we did that, we rewrote the whole column parsing code instead of trying to squeeze bits of performance out of existing code.

- The profiler obscures measurements. Make sure you check with the real world.

  Our profiles gave us the wrong impression that function call cost matters. Actually, it doesn't matter. The profiler has its own internal upkeep cost. For that reason, it's important to confirm optimization by measuring your program's execution time without the profiler.

## CHAPTER 6

Profile Memory

As we've seen, the 80-20 rule of Ruby application optimization says that 80% of performance improvements come from memory optimization. So now that you know profiling basics, I'll show you how to profile memory.

Unlike with CPU profiling, you can't simply use ruby-prof to profile memory out of the box. You'll need to have a patched Ruby interpreter for that. An alternative is to print measurements from GC#stat or GC::Profiler yourself. We'll discuss both approaches in this section.

Detect Excessive Memory Usage

But before we get to that, let's talk about how to determine that memory usage is in fact a problem in your application. For that you'll need two kinds of tools: one for monitoring and one for profiling.

No matter where you deploy, on servers or on customers' workstations, you'll need a monitoring tool to show your application's memory usage. In the Ruby on Rails world the go-to monitoring tool is New Relic.[1] Some deployment platforms, such as Heroku, have their own monitoring. If you prefer to set up your own solution, tools are available for that too. Good examples are Nagios[2] and Munin.[3]

So what can a monitoring tool show you? Something like this:

---

1. http://newrelic.com
2. http://www.nagios.org
3. http://munin-monitoring.org

That's the Heroku memory metric chart. You can see that once the application starts, its memory usage constantly grows over the course of the next few hours. When it reaches 512 MB, Heroku restarts the application, and then the growth happens again. This all definitely smells, either like a memory leak or a memory-intensive operation on the large dataset.

Should you see something like that happening for your application, your first task would be to investigate what takes that memory. So next we'll talk about the two tools you can use for that.

Profile Memory with Valgrind Massif

Valgrind[4] is a profiler for C and C++ programs that collects different data depending on the "tool" that you use. For example, Memcheck records memory leaks, Callgrind records execution times (in the same way ruby-prof does), Massif records heap usage, and so on.

Valgrind Massif produces a chart showing heap usage over time, including information about which parts of the program are responsible for the most memory allocations. Raw Massif output is not human readable, so again you'll need a visualization tool. The best multiplatform one is ms_print, which is included in the Valgrind suite. The best third-party tool is Massif Visualizer.[5] The latter works on Linux, with packages available for major distributions, and on Mac OS via my Homebrew KDE tap.[6]

Let me show you a sample Massif profile for our—already optimized—application from the previous chapter. But first let's strip everything related to testing and ruby-prof profiling from it. The program should look like this:

chp6/app_optimized4.rb
```ruby
require 'date'

# This generates CSV like
# 1, John McTest, 1980-07-01
# 2, Peter McGregor, 1985-12-23
# 3, Sylvia McIntosh, 1989-06-13
def generate_test_data
```

---

4. http://valgrind.org/
5. https://projects.kde.org/projects/extragear/sdk/massif-visualizer
6. https://github.com/adymo/homebrew-kde

```ruby
  50000.times.map do |i|
    name = ["John", "Peter", "Sylvia"][rand(3)] + " " +
           ["McTest", "McGregor", "McIntosh"][rand(3)]
    [i, name, Time.at(rand * Time.now.to_i).strftime("%Y-%m-%d") ].join(',')
  end.join("\n")
end

def parse_data(data)
  data.split("\n").map! { |row| parse_row(row) }
end

def parse_row(row)
  col1, col2, col3 = row.split(",")
  [
      col1.to_i,
      col2,
      Date.new(col3[0,4].to_i, col3[5,2].to_i, col3[8,2].to_i)
  ]
end

def find_youngest(people)
  people.map! { |person| person[2] }.max
end

data = generate_test_data
people = parse_data(data)
find_youngest(people)
```

One more thing. You can only run native executables in Valgrind. So if you are using rbenv or any other wrapper script like me, you'll need to extract from it the full path to the Ruby executable.

```
$ valgrind --tool=massif `rbenv which ruby` app_optimized4.rb
==17814== Massif, a heap profiler
==17814== Copyright (C) 2003-2013, and GNU GPL'd, by Nicholas Nethercote
==17814== Using Valgrind-3.10.0 and LibVEX; rerun with -h for copyright info
==17814== Command: ~/.rbenv/versions/2.2.0/bin/ruby app_optimized4.rb
==17814==
==17814==
```

This will produce the output file named massif.out.PID. In my case, it's called massif.out.17814. Massif prints out the process identifier (PID) of the program it profiles to the console, so be sure to look at that to locate the correct profile.

Let's open our profile in Massif Visualizer. The result is shown in the screenshot on page 88.

What we see here is a memory consumption chart for the duration of program execution plus a series of snapshots that Massif takes periodically. Each snapshot records how much memory the program has used at the time. Some

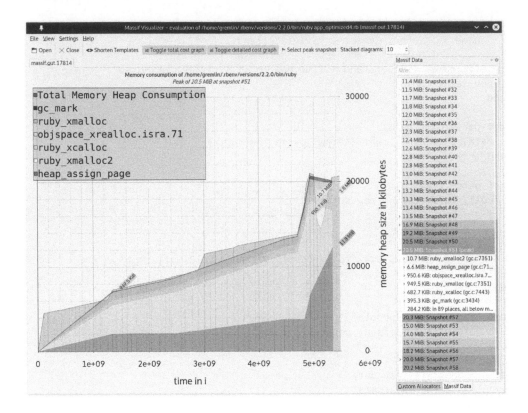

of the snapshots are detailed and include a call stack, so you can figure out which part of the code took the most memory. Unfortunately, you will see only C/C++ functions in the stack. Even though Valgrind can't dig into the Ruby code, you still can figure out what happens there. Let's look closely at one such snapshot.

Particularly interesting is a peak snapshot that I highlighted in the screenshot. In the following image on page 89 you'll see the call stack from the Massif Data view.

The first thing we see here is that our code doesn't use that much memory, peaking only at 21 MB. Roughly half of that stores our unparsed and parsed data. You will see it under the ruby_xmalloc2 branch. Most of the remaining half of the memory is the Ruby object heap, the heap_assign_page branch.

Looking through the Ruby internals stack can be daunting at first. But if you know even a bit about Ruby internals, some of which you'll learn about later in this book in Chapter 10, *Tune Up the Garbage Collector*, on page 149, you should be able to figure it out. For example, how do we know that

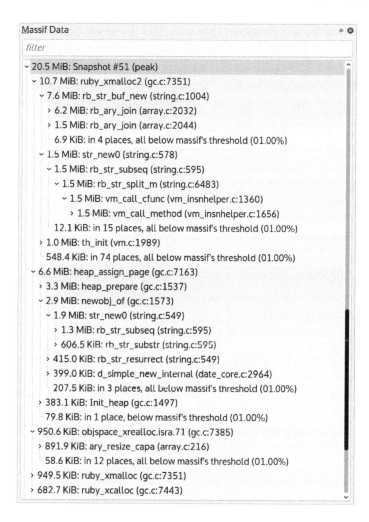

heap_page_allocate represents Ruby object creation? Because we see a newobj_of call beneath it, and we know that Ruby stores objects in its own heap.

The ruby_xmalloc2 branch is even more obvious. Inside it we only see what looks like constructor calls for arrays of strings. We don't even have to know what exactly those internal Ruby functions do. What else can they be other than constructor calls for our unparsed and parsed data objects?

From the chart itself we see that up until snapshot #51 the memory consumption was growing linearly. If we expand that snapshot, we'll see only the functions that create arrays of strings. That is the result of the data generation that we do in the generate_test_data function.

Once data is ready, our program takes 21 MB. Next we see a drop in memory usage by about 7 MB. It looks like GC was able to reclaim some memory. Then we see the 7 MB spike again, a result of data parsing and searching for the youngest person on the list. We can't optimize data generation in our example, so if we were to optimize memory, data parsing and searching is where we'd concentrate our efforts.

Massif is a great tool for looking at memory consumption. But it lacks insight into your Ruby code, and you have to guess what happens there. It would be great to look into the Ruby call stack, wouldn't it? It turns out there's a tool that *almost* does that.

Profile Object Allocations with Stackprof

Stackprof is the Ruby tool that implements the same idea as Massif. Similar to Massif, it takes snapshots (samples in Stackprof's parlance) during the program execution, and gives you a similar chart as the result. What's the catch? It samples the number of object allocations, not memory consumption. Also, it works only with Ruby 2.1 and later.

For some programs the number of objects allocated is roughly proportional to total memory consumption. That's the case for our example. All our strings are small, fit into the Ruby object, and require no additional memory on the heap. But if your program allocates small amounts of large objects, then Stackprof will not help you with memory optimization.

Let's see what Stackprof can find in our example.

First, let's install Stackprof as a gem:

```
$ gem install stackprof
```

Now let's require it in our example and wrap the code into the StackProf.run block:

chp6/app_optimized_stackprof.rb
```
require 'rubygems'
require 'stackprof'

StackProf.run(
    mode: :object,
    out: 'stackprof-object-app-optimized.dump',
    raw: true) do
  data = generate_test_data
  people = parse_data(data)
  find_youngest(people)
end
```

After we run the program it will create the stackprof-object-app-optimized.dump file with profiling results. It's a binary file that requires us to use the visualization tools that Stackprof has.

The plain-text report aggregates object allocation data either for the whole program or for any given function. Look at the report for our example program:

```
$ stackprof stackprof-object-app-optimized.dump --text
```

```
==================================
  Mode: object(1)
  Samples: 6149204 (0.00% miss rate)
  GC: 0 (0.00%)
==================================
    TOTAL     (pct)     SAMPLES    (pct)     FRAME
  5599193   (91.1%)     5599193   (91.1%)    block in Object#generate_test_data
   500000    (8.1%)      500000    (8.1%)    Object#parse_row
   550003    (8.9%)       50003    (0.8%)    Object#parse_data
  5599199   (91.1%)           6    (0.0%)    Object#generate_test_data
        2    (0.0%)           2    (0.0%)    Object#find_youngest
  6149204  (100.0%)           0    (0.0%)    block in main
  6149204  (100.0%)           0    (0.0%)    main
  6149204  (100.0%)           0    (0.0%)    main
   500000    (8.1%)           0    (0.0%)    block in Object#parse_data
```

Here 90% of all object allocations happen when we generate the test data. Parsing takes the rest. And only two allocations happen inside the find_youngest function that returns the program output.

So by looking at the Stackprof output you can determine which functions to optimize to reduce the memory consumption. In our example these are clearly Object#generate_test_data and Object#parse_row.

You can also dig deeper into the functions and see which lines generate too many objects. For example, let's look at the Object#parse_row.

```
$ stackprof stackprof-object-app-optimized.dump\
  --text --method "Object#parse_row"
```

```
samples:  500000 self (8.1%)  /   500000 total (8.1%)
callers:
  500000  (  100.0%)  block in Object#parse_data
code:
                                | 19 | def parse_row(row)
 250000 (4.1%) / 250000 (4.1%)  | 20 |   col1, col2, col3 = row.split(",")
                                | 21 |   [
  50000  (0.8%) /  50000 (0.8%) | 22 |     col1.to_i,
                                | 23 |     col2,
 200000 (3.3%) / 200000 (3.3%)  | 24 |     Date.new(...)
                                | 25 |   ]
```

Here date object creation is the biggest offender, with type conversion coming second.

There are more ways to visualize Stackprof data. For example, you can generate the HTML page with the *flame graph*. This is what Massif Visualizer does for Massif profiles.

The process of generating a flame graph may be a bit confusing. Once we have a Stackprof dump, we need to generate a JavaScript file with flame graph data:

```
$ stackprof stackprof-object-app-optimized.dump\
  --flamegraph > stackprof-object-app-optimized-flamegraph.js
```

Then we get a link to the HTML page that does visualization:

```
$ stackprof stackprof-object-app-optimized.dump\
  --flamegraph-viewer stackprof-object-app-optimized-flamegraph.js
open file:///path_to_stackprof/viewer.html?data=
  /path_to_book/chp6/stackprof-object-app-optimized-flamegraph.js
```

Finally, we copy the link from the output and open it in the browser.

Unlike with Massif, it's OK to use Stackprof in production. It's built on top of rb_profile_frames(), a C API for fetching Ruby backtraces. The API performs no allocations and adds minimal CPU overhead. So unlike Massif or ruby-prof, which slow us down by 2–10 times, Stackprof is safe to use in a live system.

Massif only tells us when and where, approximately, memory gets used. Sometimes we'll be able to guess what takes memory. Stackprof may point at the actual location in the code that takes the memory. But that only works if we're allocating too many objects, and it won't be useful if we allocate just a few heavy objects. In practice, to understand and fix the problem we'll need to dig deeper. There are better tools for that, so let's look at the available options next.

Profile Memory with Ruby-Prof

We can use the ruby-prof profiler for memory optimization too. We can ask it to measure either the size or the number of memory allocations, get a profile similar to those we saw earlier, and visualize it with the same tools. Even the approach to memory profiling is going to be similar. But there's one catch: we'll need a patched Ruby interpreter for memory profiling to work. Why? Because Ruby doesn't give the profiler enough information about memory allocation by default—exactly for performance reasons.

If you aren't adventurous enough to patch and recompile Ruby, you can skip this section and go directly to the next one, where I'll explain how to incorporate memory measurements into your code. If you're still with me here, I have good news. It's not that hard to get the patched Ruby, at least on development boxes.

Memory profiling patches are included in the RailsExpress patch set[7] maintained by Stefan Kaes along with other performance-related patches. I won't describe the whole patch set, but be sure to look at it. You may find some of those patches useful.

We'll continue to use rbenv here. We can compile Ruby with RailsExpress patches with both rbenv and rvm. The former needs an additional plug-in[8] with build scripts that I wrote and maintain. If you, like me, use rbenv, install the plug-in now.

At this point we've installed the plug-in, and rbenv install -l will show us which RailsExpress versions we can install.

```
$ rbenv install -l | grep railsexpress
    1.9.3-p551-railsexpress
    2.0.0-p598-railsexpress
    2.1.5-railsexpress
$ rbenv install -k 1.9.3-p551-railsexpress
$ rbenv install -k 2.0.0-p598-railsexpress
$ rbenv install -k 2.1.5-railsexpress
```

These versions were the latest as of this writing. Run rbenv install -l to find the latest available patched Ruby version for you.

Also make sure you have ruby-prof gem installed for all patched Rubys:

```
$ rbenv shell 1.9.3-p551-railsexpress
$ gem install ruby-prof
```

As of this writing, memory profiling patches work only with Ruby 1.8.7, 1.9.3, and 2.0.0; they don't support 2.1 and 2.2. When patches don't work, you get a memory profile with all measurements equal to zero. Try memory profiling the simple application with your Ruby version and see whether you get the results.

If you use Ruby 2.1 or 2.2, try memory profiling your app under 2.0. These versions are mostly compatible and differ only by the garbage collector. That difference has no effect on most types of memory profiling.

---

7.   https://github.com/skaes/rvm-patchsets
8.   https://github.com/adymo/ruby-build-railsexpress

Now that you have a working memory profiling config, let's explore memory profiling. Here's an extremely simple program that allocates a 10 MB string in memory and then transforms it to uppercase.

```
chp6/memprof_app.rb
require 'rubygems'
require 'ruby-prof'
require 'benchmark'

exit(0) unless ARGV[0]

GC.enable_stats
RubyProf.measure_mode = RubyProf.const_get(ARGV[0])

result = RubyProf.profile do

  str = 'x'*1024*1024*10
  str.upcase

end

printer = RubyProf::FlatPrinter.new(result)
printer.print(File.open("#{ARGV[0]}_profile.txt", "w+"), min_percent: 1)

printer = RubyProf::CallTreePrinter.new(result)
printer.print(File.open("callgrind.out.memprof_app", "w+"))
```

When profiling your application, don't forget to call the GC.enable_stats function before profiling as we did in this example. Otherwise all your measurements will be zero.

Ruby-prof comes with four memory profiling modes:

- RubyProf::MEMORY measures the total memory usage.

- RubyProf::ALLOCATIONS measures the number of object allocations.

- RubyProf::GC_RUNS measures the number of GC runs.

- RubyProf::GC_TIME measures the GC time.

Our program takes memory profiling mode as an argument and produces the flat profile named by that mode. So, let's look at what profiles we can get from all these modes.

Profile Total Memory Usage

This profile will show you how much memory your program allocates and where. This is the most important report because there's a direct relationship between the memory usage, number of garbage runs, and performance.

Joe asks:

Should I Disable GC During Memory Profiling?

No, we disabled GC for CPU profiling because it adds extra time to random places. But garbage collection neither allocates extra objects nor uses additional memory in a way that the profiler can detect, so it doesn't have any effect on memory profiles. And for some profiles like GC runs and time, we even have to keep GC turned on.

Let's run the example program and look at the report. This examples uses Ruby 1.9.3 since it's supported best by RailsExpress memory patches.

```
$ rbenv shell 1.9.3-p551-railsexpress
$ ruby memprof_app.rb MEMORY
```

Here's the report—yours might have slightly different numbers.

```
Thread ID: 4082460
Fiber ID: 5403500
Total: 21508.534180
Sort by: self_time

  %self       total       self      wait     child   calls  name
  52.38   11265.339  11265.339     0.000     0.000       3  String#*
  47.61   10240.337  10240.337     0.000     0.000       1  String#upcase

* indicates recursively called methods
```

The flat profile measures memory usage in kilobytes. As we'd expect, the program takes slightly more than 10 MB during the large string creation, and 10 MB more to do string replacement.

Note that the numbers we see in the profiler represent *only new memory allocated and used in any given function.* This has no relation to the current memory usage during the function execution. The profiler shows you neither how much memory the garbage collector reclaimed nor how much memory was allocated before the function was called. The only way to know current memory usage is to ask the operating system.

For optimization, the current memory usage is less relevant than the amount of additional memory used by a function. Even if you temporarily allocate 100 MB to do some operation, you still create 100 MB worth of work for the garbage collector. Current memory usage might have a peak, but only if you allocate more than the current Ruby heap size. Often in production you won't see the peak at all, and your code will keep being slow until you optimize those 100 MB.

You now understand what you see in the profile. So let's optimize memory.

As you'll recall from *Modify Strings in Place*, on page 16, we can modify our string in place to reduce the memory consumption. Let's do that and reprofile.

chp6/memprof_app_optimized.rb

```
require 'rubygems'
require 'ruby-prof'
require 'benchmark'

exit(0) unless ARGV[0]

GC.enable_stats
RubyProf.measure_mode = RubyProf.const_get(ARGV[0])

result = RubyProf.profile do

  str = 'x'*1024*1024*10
  str.upcase!

end

printer = RubyProf::FlatPrinter.new(result)
printer.print(File.open("#{ARGV[0]}_optimized_profile.txt", "w+"),
  min_percent: 1)
```

This is how the profile looks for the optimized program:

chp6/MEMORY_optimized_profile.txt

```
Thread ID: 3407160
Fiber ID: 4578980
Total: 11269.050781
Sort by: self_time

 %self     total      self      wait     child    calls  name
 99.97  11265.378 11265.378     0.000     0.000        3  String#*

* indicates recursively called methods
```

As expected, the program takes half as much memory. String#upcase! doesn't even appear in the profile because we've limited it to functions that take more than 1% of memory.

There's always some hidden knowledge that the profiler will reveal—especially the memory profiler. Remember iterators that allocate extra objects from Chapter 2, *Fix Common Performance Problems*, on page 13? Guess how I learned about them? By profiling a slow piece of my own code, of course. That time I profiled allocations, not memory usage. So let's see how to do that with ruby-prof.

String#gsub! Memory Consumption

Try to repeat the same profiling exercise with String#gsub and String#gsub!. You'll find that the memory profile doesn't change after optimization, meaning that String#gsub! doesn't save memory.

You can run the following program to measure the additional memory overhead of string replacement:

chp6/str_gsub_test.rb
```
str = "x"*1024*1024*10

def test(str)
  str.gsub!("x", "y")
end

measurement1 = `ps -o rss= -p #{Process.pid}`.to_i/1024
test(str)
GC.start
measurement2 = `ps -o rss= -p #{Process.pid}`.to_i/1024

puts "memory added by string replacement: #{measurement2 - measurement1}"
```

It doesn't matter whether you use String#gsub or String#gsub!; the program will report an additional 9 MB of memory caused by string replacement.

It turns out Ruby has a suboptimal implementation of gsub that doesn't really save memory. Only Ruby 2.2 fixes this bug.

Actually, using bang functions never guarantees memory savings. When you call them, you do change the state of the object. But that doesn't always mean in-place modification. That's implementation dependent.

Ruby-Prof Object Allocations

Garbage collection time increases not only with increased memory usage, but also with more allocations. If you think about it, it's natural that the more objects the garbage collector has to process, the more time it will take. Take a peek at Chapter 10, *Tune Up the Garbage Collector*, on page 149 if you can't wait to learn more about that.

Let's profile allocations in our example program before String#upcase! optimization.

```
$ rbenv shell 1.9.3-p551-railsexpress
$ ruby memprof_app.rb ALLOCATIONS
```

chp6/ALLOCATIONS_profile.txt
```
Thread ID: 15433020
Fiber ID: 16613520
Total: 7.000000
Sort by: self_time
```

```
%self      total      self       wait       child      calls  name
42.86      3.000      3.000      0.000      0.000        3    String#*
28.57      2.000      2.000      0.000      0.000        1    String#upcase
28.57      7.000      2.000      0.000      5.000        1    Global#[No method]
```

```
* indicates recursively called methods
```

In our simple case the allocations are not the problem. We create just seven objects. Two objects created in Global#[No method] are str and 'x'. String multiplication requires three more objects for each of the three "star" operators. String#upcase produces two more objects. One of them is the resulting string in uppercase. Another one is a temporary object that Ruby creates internally when the original string doesn't fit into the Ruby object and requires extra heap memory (when string length is more than 23 characters on most modern computers).

Our optimized program does exactly two allocations less.

```
$ rbenv shell 1.9.3-p551-railsexpress
$ ruby memprof_app_optimized.rb ALLOCATIONS
```

chp6/ALLOCATIONS_optimized_profile.txt
```
Thread ID: 13865760
Fiber ID: 15186560
Total: 5.000000
Sort by: self_time

%self      total      self       wait       child      calls  name
60.00      3.000      3.000      0.000      0.000        3    String#*
40.00      5.000      2.000      0.000      3.000        1    Global#[No method]
```

```
* indicates recursively called methods
```

There's no line for String#upcase! in the profile. That's because it doesn't need any extra memory.

I keep saying that it's best to use less memory and create fewer objects so that garbage collection has less work to do. So why don't we measure the number of GC runs and time directly? Let's see.

Ruby-Prof GC Runs and Times

Yes, ruby-prof can measure the number of GC runs and the amount of time GC took.

```
$ rbenv shell 1.9.3-p551-railsexpress
$ ruby memprof_app.rb GC_RUNS
$ ruby memprof_app.rb GC_TIME
```

chp6/GC_RUNS_profile.txt
```
Thread ID: 9671460
Fiber ID: 10992080
Total: 3.000000
Sort by: self_time

 %self      total      self      wait     child     calls   name
 66.67      2.000     2.000     0.000     0.000        1    String#upcase
 33.33      1.000     1.000     0.000     0.000        3    String#*

* indicates recursively called methods
```

chp6/GC_TIME_profile.txt
```
Thread ID: 16753440
Fiber ID: 18074020
Total: 0.005989
Sort by: self_time

 %self      total      self      wait     child     calls   name
 62.35      0.004     0.004     0.000     0.000        1    String#upcase
 37.65      0.002     0.002     0.000     0.000        3    String#*

* indicates recursively called methods
```

Why didn't we start by measuring those in the first place? It seems that these numbers are exactly what we need to know—except that they aren't. Ruby GC is an adaptive system. It adjusts its settings during the program runtime depending on current memory usage, memory allocation pattern, age of allocated objects, original GC settings, and many other factors.

This means that we need to replicate the same program's state in memory before each profiling session in order to expose the same GC behavior. That is of course not possible except in the simplest cases. Any production application is guaranteed to be in a different state in memory before running the same piece of code that we're trying to profile. And the same code that triggers GC several times in one case may not trigger it at all in another.

That's why the numbers of GC runs and time are useless for optimization. We should optimize the memory usage instead because it doesn't change no matter when the code is executed.

Visualize Memory Profile with KCachegrind

We can visualize all memory profiles with KCachegrind in the same way as CPU profiles. The optimization process is also the same, and will look exactly like the one we went through earlier in this chapter. Let's look at the unoptimized app memory profile in KCachegrind.

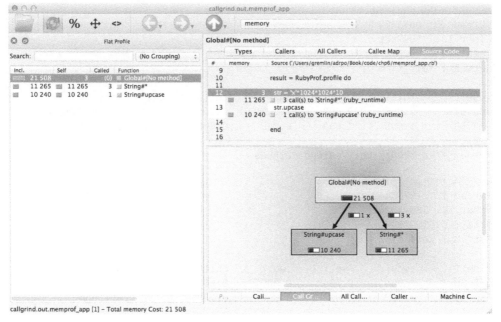

callgrind.out.memprof_app [1] – Total memory Cost: 21 508

As you can see, it's the same information that we saw in the flat text report from ruby-prof. The units (KB) are also the same.

As long as we have patched Ruby and can use it to run our application, memory profiling is easy. But what if we can't or don't want to run patched Ruby? Well, there's still one option open to us. Let's look at it next.

Measure Memory Yourself with GC#stat and GC::Profiler

You need to make manual measurements to profile memory without RailsExpress patches. We want to measure memory usage and GC statistics, print and collect them, then analyze them. That's a lot of work, but sometimes it's our only option. For example, a memory leak might happen in production only. We certainly don't want to run production inside the profiler—that would slow it down. But we can insert the measurement code instead.

The first thing we want to measure is the current memory usage. As we discussed earlier, it's less relevant than the memory usage deltas that we saw in ruby-prof, but in production, it's the only number we can get.

The best way to measure memory is to ask the operating system, as we did earlier in the book.

```
memory_before = `ps -o rss= -p #{Process.pid}`.to_i/1024
do_something
memory_after = `ps -o rss= -p #{Process.pid}`.to_i/1024
```

This of course works only on Unix operating systems.

A multiplatform approach is to ask Ruby for the GC statistics, but as we already discussed that's even less useful than measuring current memory usage. But if we have reproducible high memory usage or a leak in production, we can definitely collect GC statistics to get an idea of what happens there.

You can get GC statistics in one of two ways. You can manually collect data by calling GC#stat in several places in your code. Or you can use GC::Profiler, available in Ruby 1.9.3 and later. Let me show you both in an irb session.

```
2.1.4 :001 > GC.stat
=> {:count=>7, :heap_used=>81, :heap_length=>81, :heap_increment=>0,
    :heap_live_slot=>32578, :heap_free_slot=>438,
    :heap_final_slot=>0, :heap_swept_slot=>19535,
    :heap_eden_page_length=>81, :heap_tomb_page_length=>0,
    «...»
    :oldmalloc_increase=>2162848, :oldmalloc_limit=>16777216}
2.1.4 :002 > x = "x"*1024*1024*100; nil  # allocate 100 MB of memory
=> nil
2.1.4 :003 > GC.stat
=> {:count=>9, :heap_used=>81, :heap_length=>81, :heap_increment=>0,
    :heap_live_slot=>12785, :heap_free_slot=>20231,
    :heap_final_slot=>0, :heap_swept_slot=>20479,
    :heap_eden_page_length=>81, :heap_tomb_page_length=>0,
    «...»
    :oldmalloc_increase=>4776, :oldmalloc_limit=16777216 }
2.1.4 :004 > GC::Profiler.enable
2.1.4 :005 > y = "y"*1024*1024*100; nil  # allocate another 100 MB of memory
=> nil
2.1.4 :006 > GC::Profiler.report
GC 10 invokes.
Index Invoke Time(sec) Use Size(b) Total Size(b) Total Object GC Time(ms)
    1            0.171       505320       1321920         33048        0.755
=> nil
2.1.4 :007 > GC::Profiler.disable
=> nil
```

Here we've allocated a 100 MB string twice and measured GC statistics first with GC#stat, then with GC::Profiler.

To fully understand all the numbers reported by GC#stat you need to know the Ruby GC architecture. We'll look at that later in Chapter 10, *Tune Up the Garbage Collector*, on page 149. But even without knowing the internals, you can see that the GC count increased from 7 to 9, meaning that Ruby called the garbage collector twice during the string allocation. We also allocated more objects on the Ruby heap, but not enough to increase it. The heap still has 81 slots, with more than half of them free. The 100 MB of memory we allocated went to the operating system heap and wasn't reported here.

GC::Profiler gives us the same information but in a human-readable form. Instead of heap slots numbers we see bytes. We also get GC time. In our case GC was invoked ten times. Nine of them happened before GC::Profiler, and one during profiling. Our example doesn't create a lot of new Ruby objects, so heap usage and total size don't interest us. GC time does. As you see, the single collection pass took almost 800 ms. That's huge, and it's definitely something we'd want to optimize if it were production code.

Takeaways

1. Memory profiling is harder than CPU profiling (mostly because the tools are immature), but it can reveal more severe slowdowns. The more you use memory, the more time your program spends in garbage collection.

2. You can use ruby-prof and KCachegrind tools for memory profiling, but you need to run a patched Ruby. Fortunately, it's easy to do so with rbenv and rvm.

3. Remember the little details that can make your profiles invalid. Turn off GC for CPU profiling, but leave it on for memory profiling, especially GC calls/time profiling.

4. Don't use current memory usage and GC statistics for memory profiling unless you have no other choice. Those numbers are a function of current program state and GC settings; they aren't repeatable in production. Optimize memory allocation instead.

Profiling is hard and intimidating when you first do it. I showed you some pitfalls—expect more. The good news is that once you're comfortable profiling, you'll start to find performance gems. Remember the Ruby iterators that allocate additional objects? Or String#gsub! that doesn't really save any memory? I found these during my profiling sessions. You'll make your own discoveries, which will make up for all your struggles with the profiler.

Now that you know how to optimize with the profiler, it's time to step back and focus on measurement. We've measured execution time and memory usage before and after optimization. But did we do it right? The next chapter will answer that question.

CHAPTER 7

Measure

So far I've avoided talking too much about measurements, despite their obvious importance to optimization. Why? Because in most cases people get it right. Your intuition nudges you to run the code several times, measure results, and pick the most commonly seen measurement.

This is a viable approach, and it should yield meaningful results most of the time. But if you get your measurements wrong, your optimization will go wrong too. You may either miss the small speedup, or falsely believe in ten times optimization where in fact there is none.

So let's think about what can go wrong with measurements and how to deal with it.

External factors are the first issue that comes to mind. These might be processes running in parallel on the same machine, or unexpected swapping, or even CPU frequency management capping the system performance.

But your application internals can also affect measurements. Earlier we saw that to profile execution time you must turn off GC. Otherwise you'll see random slowdowns in unexpected places—in the same way disk operations, or other system calls in your code, may lead to nondeterministic results.

Finally, it is impossible to exclude all external and internal factors. So your measurements will vary when repeated. It can be hard in this case to compare sets of before and after optimization numbers because they will be just slightly different or even overlap.

So, let's talk about all these issues and see what we can do to obtain valid measurements and compare them correctly.

Minimize External Factors

It's obvious that before measuring performance you need to free up memory, ensure that nothing else runs in parallel, and that no disk I/O happens. But there are a few things you might want to do beyond that.

Disable Dynamic CPU Frequency Scaling

The first thing to consider is disabling dynamic CPU frequency scaling, not because scaling makes your program run slower, but because two separate program runs may be incomparable because they're executed with the CPU capped at different frequencies. That's why it's a good idea to disable CPU frequency scaling if you can.

On Linux, the *governor* defines the current CPU frequency. By default the ondemand governor is used, meaning that CPU speed will change dynamically depending on the load. You can check which governor your system runs with the cpupower tool.

```
$ cpupower frequency-info
analyzing CPU 0:
hardware limits: 1.20 GHz - 2.67 GHz
available cpufreq governors: ondemand, performance
current policy: frequency should be within 1.20 GHz and 2.67 GHz.
                The governor "ondemand" may decide which speed to use
                within this range.
current CPU frequency is 1.20 GHz.
```

These are the frequency stats for my laptop. It doesn't have much to do while I'm just typing this text, so the ondemand governor scales my CPU down to a leisurely 1.20 GHz.

If you're on Linux, you can ask the cpupower tool to set the performance governor that will force CPU to its maximum frequency.

```
$ sudo cpupower frequency-set -g performance
Setting cpu: 0
Setting cpu: 1
Setting cpu: 2
Setting cpu: 3
$ cpupower frequency-info
analyzing CPU 0:
hardware limits: 1.20 GHz - 2.67 GHz
available cpufreq governors: ondemand, performance
current policy: frequency should be within 1.20 GHz and 2.67 GHz.
                The governor "performance" may decide which speed to use
                within this range.
current CPU frequency is 2.67 GHz.
```

Windows has an analog to Linux's governor called the *power plan*. The default power plan is Balanced, similar to ondemand on Linux. You can change it to High performance in the Windows Control Panel.[1]

There's no easy way to disable CPU power management features on Mac OS. You might have to Google. There are solutions that work for some people.

Note on Intel Turbo Boost

Dynamic frequency scaling is controlled by your operating system. But Intel CPUs equipped with Turbo Boost technology can scale the frequency themselves. Based on demand they increase CPU frequency for as long as possible without overheating.

Turbo Boost has the same effect on measurements: two separate program runs may become incomparable because of differences in CPU frequency.

There are tools to disable Turbo Boost. On Linux you'd simply use cpupower frequency-set -f [desired frequency] to fixate the CPU frequency. On Windows the trick is to set CPU speed at 99% in Control Panel.[a] On the Mac there's a Turbo Boost Switcher app.[b]

a. http://superuser.com/questions/627665/how-to-disable-intel-turbo-boost-on-my-dell-laptop-with-i5-processor
b. https://github.com/rugarciap/Turbo-Boost-Switcher

Disabling dynamic CPU frequency will make your measurements more deterministic, but don't spend too much time on it if none of the tools and tricks I've described work for you. A bit of statistical analysis will help you make sense out of your measurements anyway.

Warm It Up

Another thing you should be aware of is a "cold" state. Alternative Ruby implementations running on a virtual machine (VM), like JRuby and Rubinius, require warm-up before they can produce their best results. If you run one of these, be sure to estimate how many times you need to execute the same code before the VM warms up. This number depends on code complexity, and can be as small as 10 times and as large as 10,000 times.

Even if you're running MRI, you can still run into the cold state problems with third-party software. Let's take, for example, the PostgreSQL database server.

PostgreSQL relies on the filesystem cache to keep data in memory after first access. Given enough memory, all data you ever touch will eventually end up

---

1.   See, for example, http://aps2.toshiba-tro.de/kb0/HTD12017W0001R01.htm

being cached. We all know that disk I/O is slow. This means that your Ruby application performance will be radically different depending on whether or not your data is cached.

Unlike in the previous case with alternative Rubys, here you should be really interested in both cold and warm state performance. There's no guarantee your data will always remain cached, so you must measure both states.

To get to the warm state you can just execute the same code twice. But getting a predictable cold state requires cleaning the filesystem cache. Here's the trick that works on Linux:

```
sudo echo 3 | sudo tee /proc/sys/vm/drop_caches
```

Make Internals Behave Predictably

Two things in our applications can randomly slow it down: GC and system calls. (I/O is the most common case of a system call.)

I can imaging you sighing, "Oh no, not GC again." But in this case it's easy to neutralize its effect on measurements, in one of two ways.

First, it's sometimes OK to disable GC completely before measurement. If raw performance of our code is what we're interested in, then it's absolutely fine to do that.

If we want our measurement to be closer to the real world, we can try to make GC as predictable as possible by forcing it before executing the code, like this:

```
GC.start
measurement = Benchmark.realtime do
  ...
end
```

This way our code will trigger GC in the same manner every time we run the Benchmark.realtime block.

But beware of the pitfall here. We'll have to run that code several times in order to obtain the proper measurement. If we do that by restarting the application, we'll be fine. But in a loop, as in the following code snippet, this will result in an incorrect measurement.

```
100.times do
  GC.start
  measurement = Benchmark.realtime do
    ..
  end
end
```

Why would the measurements be incorrect even though we run GC.start before each benchmark block? Because our code will allocate memory for either Ruby objects or their data. So GC will have to deal with more objects on the Ruby heap and more data on the system heap. This way, after each iteration GC time will tend to increase, thus increasing the execution time that we measure.

On Linux, Mac OS X, or any other Unix-based system, we can fix it by forking the code before the measurement:

```
100.times do
  GC.start
  pid = fork do
    GC.start
    measurement = Benchmark.realtime do
      ..
    end
  end
end
Process::waitpid(pid)
```

Forking ensures that any memory allocations happen in child processes only and don't affect the parent application. This way, every child process will start in the same state, and any GC in the child will happen at (more or less) the same time.

To minimize the effect of I/O and other system calls, simply make sure the operating system is not busy with anything else and run the code several times to cache the files that you read.

Analyze and Compare Measurements Using Statistics

Despite our best efforts to isolate our code from external factors, there will still be a variation in our measurements when we run the same code over and over again. Most of the time this won't bother us. For example, if our code takes from 10 to 15 seconds before optimization and from 1 to 2 seconds after, we won't need any statistics to tell us that our optimization worked.

But sometimes things do not look as certain. For example, say we optimized the code and the execution time went down from the 120–150 ms range to the 110–130 ms range. How can we be sure that the perceived optimization of 10–20 ms is the result of our change and not some random factor?

To answer such questions, we'll need to have some way of comparing performance measurements without knowing the true performance values before and after optimization. And statistics has the tools to do exactly that. Let me show you how to use them.

Imagine we measured the performance of the same code n times before optimization and n times after optimization. Now we want to compare these two.

Let me rephrase the same question in terms of statistics. I have two samples of random independent variables x and y. The first is the performance before optimization, the second is after. The size of my sample is n. And my question is: Are these two samples significantly different?

If we knew the true values of performance before and after, the numerical measure of the optimization effect would be just the difference between them.

And it turns out we can apply the same approach to the before and after samples that have a degree of uncertainty in them. We can calculate an interval within which we can confidently state the true optimization lies. Statistics calls this interval the confidence interval. The size of that interval will depend on the chosen level of confidence. In empirical science that level is usually 95%, meaning we can be 95% sure that the true optimization will lie inside that interval.

Let's say we are subtracting the number after optimization from the number before. So if the lower bound of the confidence interval is larger than zero, then we can confidently state that the optimization worked. If the interval starts with a negative number and ends with a positive number, then we can say that our optimization does nothing. If the upper bound is lower than zero, then our optimization made things worse.

So, it's simple to reach conclusions once we find the confidence interval of the optimization. The only remaining question is how to calculate one. Let me show you the algorithm.

1. Estimate the mean of before and after performance measurements with their averages:

$$\overline{x} = \frac{\sum_i x_i}{n} \qquad\qquad \overline{y} = \frac{\sum_i y_i}{n}$$

2. Calculate the standard deviation:

$$s_x = \sqrt{\frac{\sum_i (x_i - \overline{x})^2}{n-1}} \qquad\qquad s_y = \sqrt{\frac{\sum_i (y_i - \overline{y})^2}{n-1}}$$

3. Get the difference between before and after means. That would be the mean of our optimization:

$$\overline{x} - \overline{y}$$

4. Calculate the standard error of the difference, or in other words, the standard deviation of the optimization:

$$s_{\overline{x} - \overline{y}} = \sqrt{\frac{s_x^2}{n} + \frac{s_y^2}{n}}$$

5. Finally, obtain the 95% confidence interval of the optimization. That is roughly two standard deviations away from its mean:

$$(\overline{x} - \overline{y}) \pm 2 * s_{\overline{x} - \overline{y}}$$

We want the lower bound of the interval to be larger than 0. So for example, this interval proves we indeed optimized our code:

$$0.05 \pm 0.02$$

The true difference between before and after values lies in the interval from 0.03 to 0.07 seconds. So in this imaginary case we optimized at least 30 ms.

It might seem that there's no point in calculating the confidence interval if the difference of the means is negative. But remember, we also want to know whether the optimization made things worse. For example, consider the intervals -0.05 ± 0.08 and -0.05 ± 0.02.

In both cases optimization didn't work. But in the second case it made things worse. The upper bound of the interval is -0.03. This means that with 95% confidence we can state that the code slowed down after the change, and the "optimization" must be reverted.

If you are more statistically inclined, you might frown at my confidence interval analysis. Yes, that is a shortcut, but a useful one. Of course, if you would like to be more rigorous, you can apply any of the hypothesis tests to make sure the optimization was significant. If you took 30 measurements or more, you can use the z-test. Otherwise, the t-test should work. I won't talk about these tests here because the confidence interval analysis should be good enough.

OK. Enough of formulas. It's time for an example.

The following calculates the product of the numeric array values in an idiomatic Ruby way:

chp7/before.rb
```
require 'benchmark'

data = Array.new(100000) { 10 }

GC.start
time = Benchmark.realtime do
  product = data.inject(1) { |product, i| product * i }
end
puts time
```

As we already know from Chapter 2, the inject iterator can be bad for performance. So we optimize by replacing it with each and calculating the product ourselves.

chp7/after.rb
```
require 'benchmark'

data = Array.new(100000) { 10 }

GC.start
time = Benchmark.realtime do
  product = 1
  data.each do |value|
    product *= value
  end
end
puts time
```

Let's run our before and after examples ten times each. That's not enough to make statistically sound conclusions, but we'll still do this for the sake of brevity. To make our statistics work we should take, as a rule of thumb, more than 30 measurements.

Before optimization:

```
$ for i in {1..10}; do    \
    ruby chp7/before.rb; \
  done
1.4879834910097998
1.4997473749972414
1.4694619810034055
1.4671519770054147
1.4394851910183206
1.4421958939929027
1.528489818010712
1.4666885799961165
1.4510531660052948
1.4629958330187947
```

After optimization:

```
$ for i in {1..10}; do \
    ruby chp7/after.rb; \
  done
1.4609190789924469
1.5091172570013441
1.4735914790071547
1.4498213600018062
1.445483470975887
1.46490533000906
1.434979079987388
1.4596990160061978
1.4734973890008405
1.4513041169848293
```

Just looking at the numbers it's impossible to tell whether the optimization worked. So let's use statistics.

But before we do that, we need to round our numbers off. They contain too many non-significant figures. Ruby's Benchmark#realtime that we use for measurements uses the operating system clock. That has microsecond precision in most cases, so we'll round our results to that.

Here are the rules for rounding to significant figures:

- If the first non-significant figure is a 5 followed by other non-zero digits, round up the last significant figure (away from zero).

  For example, 1.2459 as the result of a measurement that only allows for three significant figures should be written 1.25.

- If the first non-significant figure is a 5 not followed by any other digits or followed only by zeros, rounding requires a tie-breaking rule. For our case, use the "round half to even" rule, which rounds to the nearest even number.

  For example, to round 1.25 to two significant figures, round down to 1.2. To round 1.35, you should instead round up to 1.4.

- If the first non-significant figure is more than 5, round up the last significant figure.

- If the first non-significant figure is less than 5, just truncate the non-significant figures.

Once you start rounding to significant figures, you must continue doing so for all subsequent results of calculations.

Let's follow the rules and round our measurements to significant figures.

Before optimization:	After optimization:
1.487983	1.460919
1.499747	1.509117
1.469462	1.473591
1.467152	1.449821
1.439485	1.445483
1.442196	1.464905
1.528490	1.434979
1.466689	1.459699
1.451053	1.473497
1.462996	1.451304

Now let's follow our algorithm to get the optimization mean and its confidence interval.

1. Averages of the before and after performance measurements:

$$\overline{x} = \frac{1.487983 + 1.499747 + \cdots}{10} = 1.471525$$

$$\overline{y} = \frac{1.460919 + 1.509117 + \cdots}{10} = 1.462332$$

2. The standard deviation of the measurements:

$$s_x = \sqrt{\frac{(1.487983 - 1.471525)^2 + (1.499747 - 1.471525)^2 + \cdots}{9}} = 0.027361$$

$$s_y = \sqrt{\frac{(1.460919 - 1.462332)^2 + (1.509117 - 1.462332)^2 + \cdots}{9}} = 0.020456$$

3. The mean of our optimization:

$$1.471525 - 1.462332 = 0.009193$$

4. The standard deviation of the optimization:

$$s_{\overline{x} - \overline{y}} = \sqrt{\frac{0.027361^2}{10} + \frac{0.020456^2}{10}} = 0.010803$$

5. The 95% confidence interval of the optimization:

$$0.009193 \pm 2 * 0.010803 = (-0.012413, 0.030799)$$

What's the conclusion? With 95% confidence we can say that our optimization didn't work. Or, more exactly, we can't tell whether or not it worked. The difference between the inject and each iterators was not significant enough for this example.

Now let's take another look at the optimization mean and the confidence interval. The mean of our optimization was positive, about 9 ms. What invalidated our result is the standard deviation. Because it was too large, the 95% confidence interval is around plus/minus 20 ms.

What if we could reduce the variability in measurements? That would decrease the standard deviation, and, in turn, the confidence interval would be shorter. Can it be that with more precise measurements the confidence interval would lie above zero? Absolutely! That's why we spent so much time in the first part of this chapter to reduce the effect of various external and internal factors.

It is important to reduce the standard deviation of measurements as much as possible. Otherwise, you won't be able to compare your before/after results at all.

Now, in this example we are talking about milliseconds. In reality I was never able to detect such optimizations in Ruby applications. But you should definitely aim for the order of tens of milliseconds—at the very least, the lower hundreds.

You should now know enough techniques to reduce the dispersion in measurements. But if you tried them all and the standard deviation is still too high to compare results, try this: exclude outliers—measurements that are too distant from each other. Mathematicians don't like this approach, but it can help if nothing else works.

The second run of my after optimization example measured 1.509117 seconds. That was definitely an outlier. If I excluded it, both my mean and standard deviation would go down significantly.

But don't blindly exclude any results. There are a couple of statistically sound techniques of data rejection. Make sure you learn them.[2]

OK, so now you know how to compare measurements before and after optimization. Some pretty hardcore statistics are involved in that, and you probably think now, "why bother?" You'll find the answer right away in the next chapter. For now, let's summarize what you've learned.

Takeaways

There's only one way to prove that the optimization worked. You measure the performance before and after, and you compare. But the devil is in the details. Here's what you need to take care of to get the measurements right.

1. Minimize external factors to increase measurement accuracy.

2. Make sure that GC behaves as predictably as possible to decrease variability in measurements.

3. Take as many measurements as practical to make statistical analysis possible. A good default is 30.

4. Compare before and after numbers by calculating the confidence interval of the optimization effect. Conclude that optimization worked only when the lower bound of the confidence interval is higher than 0.

5. Try to reduce dispersion in measurements as much as possible. Otherwise even with statistical tools you won't be able to tell whether or not you optimized the code.

---

2. https://en.wikipedia.org/wiki/Truncation_(statistics) and https://en.wikipedia.org/wiki/Winsorising

Now we know how to do measurements, and how to compare them. But the goal of optimization is not to measure it, nor even to make sure that the optimized code indeed runs faster.

The real goal is to *optimize* and to make sure the slowdown never happens again. How can you do that? After optimization you'll need to measure the performance after every change, and detect even the smallest regressions from the achieved performance level.

If that smells like testing, you're right: it is testing. Performance testing. And that's exactly what we'll talk about in the next chapter.

CHAPTER **8**

Test Performance

As experienced software developers, we know that testing is the best way to ensure that our code works as advertised. When you first write the code, a test proves that it does what you think it does. When you fix a bug, the test prevents it from happening again.

I'm a big fan of applying the same approach for performance. What if we write tests that first set the expected level of performance, and then make sure that performance doesn't degrade below this level? Sounds like a good idea, right?

I learned about this concept while working on Acunote. We started Acunote when Rails was at version 1.0, so performance was a huge concern. Performance testing helped us not only to understand and improve application performance, but to survive through numerous Rails upgrades. It turned out that even a minor version upgrade could introduce the performance regression in some unexpected way. We wouldn't be able to detect and fix these regressions without the performance tests.

So let me show you how we did performance testing in Acunote and how you can do it too.

A unit test for a function might look something like this:

```
def test_do_something
  assert_equal 4, do_something(2,2)
end
```

This test in fact performs three separate steps: evaluation, assertion, and error reporting. Testing frameworks abstract these three steps, so we end up writing just one line of code to do all three.

To evaluate, our example test runs the do_something function to get its return value. The assertion assesses the equality of this actual value against the expected value. If the assertion fails, the test reports the error.

A performance test should perform these same three steps, but each one of them will be slightly different. Say we want to write the performance test for this same do_something function. The test will look like this:

```
def test_something_performance
  actual_performance = performance_benchmark do
    do_something(2,2))
  end
  assert_performance actual_performance
end
```

The evaluation step is simply a benchmarking. The actual value for assert_performance is the current set of the performance measurements.

Ah, but what is our expected level of performance? We said that our performance test should ensure that performance doesn't degrade below an expected level. A reasonable answer is that our assert_performance should make sure that performance is the same as or better than before. So the test should somehow know the performance measurements from the previous test run. Those measurements make up the expected value that we'll compare to. What if there are no previous results? Then the only thing the test should do is store the results for future comparison.

We already know how to compare performance measurements from the previous chapter. So the remaining thing to figure out is how and where to store the previous test results. This is something regular tests don't do.

Should the test find a slowdown, we want to the performance before and after, and their difference. As we know from the previous chapter, all before and after numbers should come with their deviations, and the difference should come with its confidence interval. This means the reporting step in performance tests is also very different from what you usually see in tests.

OK, that's the big picture of performance testing. Now, the details.

Benchmark

Let's take everything you learned in the previous chapter on measurements and apply that knowledge here to write a benchmark function. To reiterate, here's what such a function should do:

- Run the code multiple times to gather measurements. It's best if we can do 30 runs or more.

- Skip the results of the first run to reduce the warm-up effects and let caching do its job.

- Force GC before each run.

- Fork the process before measurement to make sure all runs are isolated and don't interfere with each other.

- Store all measurements somewhere (in the file, on S3, etc.) to be processed later.

- Calculate and report average performance and its standard deviation.

This list makes for a pretty detailed spec, so let's go ahead and write the benchmark function.

chp8/performance_benchmark.rb
```ruby
require 'benchmark'

def performance_benchmark(name, &block)
  # 31 runs, we'll discard the first result
  (0..30).each do |i|
    # force GC in parent process to make sure we reclaim
    # any memory taken by forking in previous run
    GC.start

    # fork to isolate our run
    pid = fork do
      # again run GC to reduce effects of forking
      GC.start
      # disable GC if you want to see the raw performance of your code
      GC.disable if ENV["RUBY_DISABLE_GC"]

      # because we are in a forked process, we need to store
      # results in some shared space.
      # local file is the simplest way to do that
      benchmark_results = File.open("benchmark_results_#{name}", "a")

      elapsed_time = Benchmark::realtime do
        yield
      end

      # do not count the first run
      if i > 0
        # we use system clock for measurements,
        # so microsecond is the last significant figure
        benchmark_results.puts elapsed_time.round(6)
      end
      benchmark_results.close

      GC.enable if ENV["RUBY_DISABLE_GC"]
    end
    Process::waitpid pid
  end
end
```

```
measurements = File.readlines("benchmark_results_#{name}").map do |value|
  value.to_f
end
File.delete("benchmark_results_#{name}")

average = measurements.inject(0) do |sum, x|
  sum + x
end.to_f / measurements.size
stddev = Math.sqrt(
  measurements.inject(0){ |sum, x| sum + (x - average)**2 }.to_f /
    (measurements.size - 1)
)

# return both average and standard deviation,
# this time in millisecond precision
# for all practical purposes that should be enough
[name, average.round(3), stddev.round(3)]
end
```

We made three simplifications in the benchmarking function. First, we used the Ruby round function that doesn't follow the tie-breaking rule of rounding when the first non-significant digit is 5 followed by 0. Instead of rounding to the nearest even number, it'll always round up. Second, we decreased precision to milliseconds despite the system clock being able to measure times with microsecond precision. Finally, we hard-coded the number of measurements to 30.

You can easily undo the first and the last simplifications, but I recommend you keep the second. Ruby isn't a systems programming language, so we usually don't care about microseconds of execution time. In fact, in most cases we don't care about milliseconds or even tens of milliseconds—that's why we rounded off our measurements in our example.

Now let's see how our benchmarking function works. Run this simple program:

chp8/test_performance_benchmark.rb
```
require 'performance_benchmark'

result = performance_benchmark("sleep 1 second") do
  sleep 1
end
puts "%-28s %0.3f ± %0.3f" % result
```

```
$ cd code/chp8
$ ruby -I . test_performance_benchmark.rb
sleep 1 second               1.000 ± 0.000
```

As expected, sleep(1) takes exactly one second, with no deviation. We can be sure our measurements are correct. Now it's time to write the function to assert the performance.

Assert Performance

We know that assert_performance should measure the current performance, compare it with the performance from the previous run, and store the current measurements as the reference value for the next run. Of course, the first test run should just store the results because there's no previous data to compare with.

Now let's think through success and failure scenarios for such tests. Failure is easy. If performance is significantly worse, then report the failure. The success scenario, though, has two possible outcomes: one when performance is not significantly different, and another when it has significantly improved.

It looks like it's not enough just to report failure/success. We need to report the current measurement, as well as any significant difference in performance.

So let's get back to the editor and try to do exactly that.

chp8/assert_performance.rb

```ruby
require 'minitest/autorun'

class Minitest::Test
  def assert_performance(current_performance)
    self.assertions += 1  # increase Minitest assertion counter

    benchmark_name, current_average, current_stddev = *current_performance
    past_average, past_stddev = load_benchmark(benchmark_name)
    save_benchmark(benchmark_name, current_average, current_stddev)

    optimization_mean, optimization_standard_error = compare_performance(
      past_average, past_stddev, current_average, current_stddev
    )

    optimization_confidence_interval = [
      optimization_mean - 2*optimization_standard_error,
      optimization_mean + 2*optimization_standard_error
    ]

    conclusion = if optimization_confidence_interval.all? { |i| i < 0 }
      :slowdown
    elsif optimization_confidence_interval.all? { |i| i > 0 }
      :speedup
    else
      :unchanged
    end
```

```ruby
    print "%-28s %0.3f ± %0.3f: %-10s" %
      [benchmark_name, current_average, current_stddev, conclusion]
    if conclusion != :unchanged
      print " by %0.3f..%0.3f with 95%% confidence" %
        optimization_confidence_interval
    end
    print "\n"

    if conclusion == :slowdown
      raise MiniTest::Assertion.new("#{benchmark_name} got slower")
    end
  end

private

  def load_benchmark(benchmark_name)
    return [nil, nil] unless File.exist?("benchmarks/#{benchmark_name}")
    benchmark = File.read("benchmarks/#{benchmark_name}")
    benchmark.split(" ").map { |value| value.to_f }
  end

  def save_benchmark(benchmark_name, current_average, current_stddev)
    File.open("benchmarks/#{benchmark_name}", "w+") do |f|
      f.write "%0.3f %0.3f" % [current_average, current_stddev]
    end
  end

  def compare_performance(past_average, past_stddev,
                          current_average, current_stddev)
    # when there's no past data, just report no performance change
    past_average ||= current_average
    past_stddev ||= current_stddev

    optimization_mean = past_average - current_average
    optimization_standard_error = (current_stddev**2/30 +
      past_stddev**2/30)**0.5

    # drop non-significant digits that our calculations might introduce
    optimization_mean = optimization_mean.round(3)
    optimization_standard_error = optimization_standard_error.round(3)

    [optimization_mean, optimization_standard_error]
  end
end
```

Again, this includes some simplifications you can easily undo. First, we save the benchmark results to the file in a predefined hard-coded location. Second, we hardcode the number of measurement repetitions to 30, exactly as in the performance_benchmark function. And third, our assert_performance works only with Minitest 5.0 and later, so we need to install the minitest gem.

But now that we have our assert, we can write our first performance test.

chp8/test_assert_performance1.rb
```ruby
require 'assert_performance'
require 'performance_benchmark'

class TestAssertPerformance < Minitest::Test

  def test_assert_performance
    actual_performance = performance_benchmark("string operations") do
      result = ""
      700.times do
        result += ("x"*1024)
      end
    end
    assert_performance actual_performance
  end

end
```

Let's run it (don't forget to gem install minitest first).

```
$ ruby -I . test_assert_performance1.rb
# Running:
string operations          0.172 ± 0.011: unchanged
.
Finished in 2.294557s, 0.4358 runs/s, 0.4358 assertions/s.
1 runs, 1 assertions, 0 failures, 0 errors, 0 skips
```

The first run will save the measurements to the benchmarks/string operations file. If we rerun the test without making any changes, it should report no change.

```
$ ruby -I . test_assert_performance1.rb
# Running:
string operations          0.168 ± 0.016: unchanged
.
Finished in 2.313815s, 0.4322 runs/s, 0.4322 assertions/s.
1 runs, 1 assertions, 0 failures, 0 errors, 0 skips
```

As expected, the test reports that performance hasn't changed despite the difference in average numbers. That's statistical analysis at work! Now you know why we spent so much time talking about it.

Now let's optimize the program. I'll take my own advice from Chapter 2 and replace String#+= with String#<<.

```
chp8/test_assert_performance2.rb
require 'assert_performance'
require 'performance_benchmark'

class TestAssertPerformance < Minitest::Test

  def test_assert_performance
    actual_performance = performance_benchmark("string operations") do
      result = ""
      700.times do
        result << ("x"*1024)
      end
    end
    assert_performance actual_performance
  end

end
```

Let's run the performance test again.

```
$ bundle exec ruby -I . test_assert_performance2.rb
# Running:
string operations 0.004 ± 0.000: speedup by 0.161..0.167 with 95% confidence
.
Finished in 1.089948s, 0.9175 runs/s, 0.9175 assertions/s.
1 runs, 1 assertions, 0 failures, 0 errors, 0 skips
```

And of course the test reports the huge optimization. That's exactly what we like to see when we optimize.

However, if the execution environment isn't perfect, our performance test might report a slowdown or optimization even if we did nothing. For example, I can get the slowdown error from the first unoptimized test on my laptop when it gets busy doing something else. This is one such test run:

```
$ ruby -I . test_assert_performance1.rb
# Running:
string operations 0.201 ± 0.059: slowdown by -0.044..-0.022 with 95% confidence
F
Finished in 2.456716s, 0.4070 runs/s, 0.4070 assertions/s.

  1) Failure:
TestAssertPerformance#test_assert_performance [test_assert_performance1.rb:10]:
string operations got slower

1 runs, 1 assertions, 1 failures, 0 errors, 0 skips
```

See how big my standard deviation is? It's almost a quarter of my average. This means that some of the measurements were outliers, and they made the test fail.

We already talked about two ways of dealing with that. One is to further minimize external factors. Another is to exclude outliers. But there's one more: you can increase the confidence level for the optimization interval.

The 95% confidence interval we use is roughly plus/minus two standard errors from the mean of the difference between before and after numbers. We can demand 99% confidence. This increases the interval to about plus/minus three standard errors.

Let's do some quick math to see whether that helps with my failing test. My before and after numbers numbers are 0.168 ± 0.016 and 0.201 ± 0.059.

The mean of the difference is

$$\overline{x} - \overline{y} = 0.168 - 0.201 = -0.033$$

The standard error of the mean of the difference is

$$s_{\overline{x}-\overline{y}} = \sqrt{\frac{0.016^2}{30} + \frac{0.059^2}{30}} = 0.011$$

The three standard error interval is (-0.066..0). This means that we can't be 99% confident that the second test run was slower or faster. So the new conclusion is that nothing has changed.

Note how simple tweaking of the confidence interval changed the test outcome. So I recommend that you play with this and come up with the confidence level that works reliably for your performance tests.

There's of course a limit to confidence level increases. See how we were barely able to determine that performance in our test stayed the same. Had the standard deviation been one millisecond less, we would have declared this run as a slowdown.

You might be tempted to increase the interval size to four or five standard errors from the mean. But in practice, three standard errors (99%) is the highest confidence you should aim for. You can't demand the confidence of the large hadron collider experiments from your Ruby tests. If your tests are still not reliable, step back and look for more external factors, or start excluding outliers in measurements.

Report Slowdowns and Optimizations

The test prints benchmarks together with any deviations from the previous runs. Is there anything else to report? Yes, but not in the test output.

A performance test is a perfect candidate for daily or continuous testing. Make sure you notify developers about any changes in performance, good or bad.

I personally take the complete output of the test and report that. It contains enough information for a human to assess performance. Your choice might be different, so I won't talk further about reporting here.

Test Rails Application Performance

If you're writing Rails applications, you'll surely want to apply the same performance testing techniques to them. Rails developers have long since recognized that. Rails 3 even included a performance testing framework. And while Rails 4 no longer provides it, the code is still there in the rails-perftest gem.[1]

So should we simply use that gem for Rails performance testing? No, not really. The rails-perftest gem tries to be the Jack of all trades and becomes the master of none. It does benchmarking and profiling, and lets you collect many metrics other than execution time.

At the same time, it doesn't do enough runs for its benchmarks to be statistically significant. And it doesn't do any comparison. And, honestly, mixing profiling with performance testing in one tool doesn't sound like a good idea.

With that in mind, I think we're better off adapting our performance_benchmark and assert_performance functions to work with Rails. So let's see what it takes.

Make Rails Performance Test an Integration Test

Rails is a complex stack of software. In the performance test we need to make sure we benchmark the complete stack, not just a part of it. It might be tempting to performance test only a controller action, or even a function in the model. But what if we add some middleware that totally ruins our performance? Will our performance test spot that?

The only kind of test that runs the whole Rails stack every request is the integration test, so let's start writing one.

```
class RailsAppPerformanceTest < ActionDispatch::IntegrationTest
  test "performance test something" do
    actual_performance = performance_benchmark do
      get "/something"
    end
    assert_performance actual_performance
  end
end
```

---

1. https://github.com/rails/rails-perftest

The good thing about this test is, again, that it processes the request almost in the same way our production application would. Ah, but the devil is in details. While the get or post calls from the integration test do execute the whole Rails stack, they do excessive logging and no caching.

By default, tests run with the :debug log level. To imitate production, we'll need to set it to :info. We can either create a separate environment for performance testing, or simply set the log level before each test like this:

```
class RailsAppPerformanceTest < ActionDispatch::IntegrationTest
  def setup
    @previous_log_level = Rails.application.config.log_level
    Rails.application.config.log_level = :info
  end
  def teardown
    Rails.application.config.log_level = @previous_log_level
  end
end
```

Caching is more complicated. If our application heavily relies on caching, we must be sure to turn it on for performance tests. Our benchmark function skips the results of the first test run, so it will correctly ignore the first, uncached, request. This means no changes to the testing infrastructure are needed: we just execute Rails.application.config.action_controller.perform_caching = true in the same place where we change the log level.

Benchmark Rails the Right Way

So we wrote an integration performance test, reduced logging, and decided on caching. Is there anything else to think about? It turns out, yes.

The majority of Rails apps work with a database. They load and store data there. When we talked about benchmarking Ruby code earlier, we didn't think about the byproducts of that code. Instead we assumed that there were no side effects and that it was safe to rerun the same function again and again.

Not so much with Rails. In most cases the time you measure will increase with each test run during the benchmark. Why? Because when you hit Rails, more often than not you change the database. This way you might end up with more and more data to process in each subsequent test run.

Say our Rails action inserts a record into the database, then returns a summary of the stored data. The more we insert, the slower our action becomes. The measurement from the 30th test run will be way different from the first. Remember what that means for performance tests? Large standard deviations in the benchmarks and large standard errors of the optimization. As a result, we won't be able to compare the performance.

So we'll need to make sure the test runs leave no byproducts. The easiest way to do that is to start a transaction, measure, and roll it back. That's exactly what Rails does in between tests. But now we'll have to do that in between measurements inside one test. Let me show you how to modify the performance_benchmark function to do that.

```ruby
chp8/rails_performance_benchmark.rb
require 'benchmark'

class PerformanceTestTransactionError < StandardError
end

def performance_benchmark(name, &block)
  # 31 runs, we'll discard the first result
  (0..30).each do |i|
    # force GC in parent process to make sure we reclaim
    # any memory taken by forking in previous run
    GC.start

    # fork to isolate our run
    pid = fork do
      # again run GC to reduce effects of forking
      GC.start
      # disable GC if you want to see the raw performance of your code
      GC.disable if ENV["RUBY_DISABLE_GC"]

      # because we are in a forked process, we need to store
      # results in some shared space.
      # local file is the simplest way to do that
      benchmark_results = File.open("benchmark_results_#{name}", "a")

      elapsed_time = nil
      begin
        ActiveRecord::Base.transaction do
          elapsed_time = Benchmark::realtime do
            yield
          end
          raise PerformanceTestTransactionError
        end
      rescue PerformanceTestTransactionError
        # rollback transaction as expected
      end

      # do not count the first run
      if i > 0
        # we use system clock for measurements,
        # so microsecond is the last significant figure
```

```
    benchmark_results.puts elapsed_time.round(6)
  end
  benchmark_results.close

  GC.enable if ENV["RUBY_DISABLE_GC"]

  # Hack! Do this only if you use database sockets.
  # dup2 all file descriptors to /dev/null so that forked process
  # forgets them and doesn't close them at exit.
  # Otherwise the forked process will close the database connection.
  3.upto(256) { |fd| IO.new(fd).reopen("/dev/null") rescue nil }
  end
  Process::waitpid pid
end

measurements = File.readlines("benchmark_results_#{name}").map do |value|
  value.to_f
end
File.delete("benchmark_results_#{name}")

average = measurements.inject(0) do |sum, x|
  sum + x
end.to_f / measurements.size
stddev = Math.sqrt(
  measurements.inject(0){ |sum, x| sum + (x - average)**2 }.to_f /
    (measurements.size - 1)
)

# return both average and standard deviation,
# this time in millisecond precision
# for all practical purposes that should be enough
[name, average.round(3), stddev.round(3)]
end
```

All it takes is to wrap your measurement into the transaction, and roll it back after you're done. Some people may need the socket hack that I highlighted in the previous example.

That's the trick I learned at Acunote. We used to develop and test on Linux, and connected to the PostgreSQL database via local sockets. If you do the same, you'll need the hack because the forked measurement process will attempt to close all its sockets at exit. And one of those sockets will be the database connection that the forked process is sharing with its parent. So after the socket is closed, the parent won't be able to continue benchmarking.

With all these modifications in place, our benchmarking function and our assertion are Rails compatible and ready to be used. So, you're good to go and write your own Rails performance test for your applications.

But before we jump into that, let me tell you about one more kind of performance test that's not applicable to most of the pure Ruby applications but that's really important for Rails.

Test Database Performance

A Rails application is not just Ruby code. With all the ActiveModel and ActiveRecord abstractions, developers tend to forget about the underlying database. But its performance is essential to the performance of the whole application.

If the queries we run are slow, the application will be slow. If we execute too many queries, the application will be slow. See the pattern? We absolutely need to take care that our performance tests account for the database performance.

We have two kinds of database-related performance problems: slow queries and too many queries. Are our performance tests helping us to prevent each of these two kinds of database slowdowns? It turns out the answer is no in both cases. What can we do about that? The answer: Generate enough data for tests in the first case, and write another kind of tests in the second. Let me explain.

Generate Enough Data for Performance Tests

Say we have an application that has a slow query. If we see that query in development mode, we'll optimize it, and write the performance test that calls the code that executes this query. Such a test will make sure the query doesn't get any slower with time. Nothing more to do here.

But what if we spot the slow query only in production? For example, we see it in the database server logs, or in the NewRelic report. This usually means our test database doesn't have enough data. Production has way more data, and that makes queries slower there.

So our best strategy is to *generate enough data for our performance tests*.

How much is enough? That depends on both our application and our data. In some cases our request only inserts data, and there's nothing we need to add to our test database.

In other cases our request processes all data from a table that, for example, contains 10,000 rows on production. Then our test database also needs 10,000 rows in that table.

Yet another case is when the request uses just 100 rows out of 10,000 total. So it might be enough to have only 100 rows prepared for the performance test. Or it might not be—for example, if our database structure lacks an index that makes fetching 100 rows out of 10,000 as fast as fetching 100 rows out of 100.

There are more cases of course, so I can't give you more specific advice here. When writing the performance test, think through the data usage and use your best judgment to generate just enough data to match the production behavior for your particular situation.

Test Database Queries

Executing slow queries is obviously bad for performance. But running too many queries is also bad.

We've seen that in the example from *Preload Aggressively*, on page 42. There, the extra 10,000 queries took an extra 250 seconds of execution time. Although realistic, that example is rather extreme. You'll surely notice this kind of slowdown before the code goes into production.

A more subtle case is when our request runs just several dozen queries. In development that might not be noticeable at all because we have less data and run everything in a single process with no concurrency. But our production environment is going to be exactly the opposite, with more data and high concurrency. So our harmless dozen queries can become a huge performance problem.

Because Rails is such a good abstraction, it's hard to understand how many queries are executed just by looking at the source code. Gems that magically do authentication, authorization, validation, and many other things completely hide the database operations from us.

The only place to see the queries executed is the development log. And, honestly, how often do you look there? In a moderately complex application the log is too verbose to parse visually, let alone to count queries.

So how do we make sure we don't run too many queries? When I worked on Acunote, we ran into the same problem. Our solution was to write what we called a *query test*.

A query test is a test that executes the snippet of code, gathers the list of SQL queries from the log, and asserts that this list hasn't changed from the previous test run. That's like a performance test that measures the number of queries instead of the execution time.

Rails 3.0 and higher makes it easy to gather the list of queries. We can simply subscribe to the sql.active_record hook of ActiveSupport::Notifications.

```
chp8/app/test/integration/query_test.rb
def track_queries
  result = []
  ActiveSupport::Notifications.subscribe "sql.active_record" do |*args|
    event = ActiveSupport::Notifications::Event.new(*args)
    query_name = event.payload[:name]
    next if ['SCHEMA'].include?(query_name) # skip AR schema lookups
    result << query_name
  end
  yield
  ActiveSupport::Notifications.unsubscribe("sql.active_record")
  result
end
```

This function will execute a block and return the list of query names. Now how do we assert that the list stays the same? We can use assert_equal, but we'd have to modify the test by hand every time we make a legitimate change that results in an additional query.

The assert_value gem[2] we wrote while working on Acunote is a better way to do that. It compares the expected value with the actual value, just like assert_equal. But when the actual value changes, it asks us to either confirm the change as legitimate or reject it as a test failure. If we confirm, it goes into the test file and updates the expected value. This turned out to be useful not only for performance testing. We ended up using assert_value for the majority of our tests in Acunote, and I now use it in all my other projects.

So let's use the assert_value to write a query test. We'll take a sample Rails application from Chapter 3 for that.

First, let's add my gem to the Gemfile:

```
gem 'assert_value', require: false
```

Second, update your bundle:

```
$ bundle install
```

Let's take the preloading example from *Preload Aggressively*, on page 42, and then write a query test for it. But first let's modify it a bit. We'll put the code into the controller action to imitate the real Rails application, and limit the number of rows to 10 for brevity. Also, our controller action will execute either the unoptimized or optimized code depending on the params.

---

2.   https://github.com/acunote/assert_value

```
chp8/app/app/controllers/application_controller.rb
class ApplicationController < ActionController::Base
  def do_something
    if params[:preload]
      Thing.limit(10).includes(:minions).load
    else
      Thing.limit(10).each { |thing| thing.minions.load }
    end
    render nothing: true
  end

end
```

We'll need a route to request that action, so we add the following line to our config/routes.rb:

```
root 'application#do_something'
```

Now let's put together everything we've talked about, and write our query test.

```
chp8/app/test/integration/query_test.rb
require 'test_helper'
require 'assert_value'

class QueryTest < ActionDispatch::IntegrationTest

  def test_loading_things
    ActiveRecord::Base.connection.execute <<-END
      insert into things(col0, col1, col2, col3, col4,
                         col5, col6, col7, col8, col9) (
        select
        rpad('x', 100, 'x'), rpad('x', 100, 'x'), rpad('x', 100, 'x'),
        rpad('x', 100, 'x'), rpad('x', 100, 'x'), rpad('x', 100, 'x'),
        rpad('x', 100, 'x'), rpad('x', 100, 'x'), rpad('x', 100, 'x'),
        rpad('x', 100, 'x')
        from generate_series(1, 10000)
      );
    END

    queries = track_queries do
      get "/"
    end
    assert_value queries
  end

private

  def track_queries
    result = []
    ActiveSupport::Notifications.subscribe "sql.active_record" do |*args|
```

```
        event = ActiveSupport::Notifications::Event.new(*args)
        query_name = event.payload[:name]
        next if ['SCHEMA'].include?(query_name) # skip AR schema lookups
        result << query_name
      end
      yield
      ActiveSupport::Notifications.unsubscribe("sql.active_record")
      result
    end

end
```

Like our previous performance tests, this query test is an integration test, and for the same reason: we need to test the complete Rails stack to be sure there are no extra queries magically added by gems and plug-ins behind our back.

So, let's run this test.

```
$ bundle exec ruby -I test test/integration/query_test.rb
```

The first time we run the test, it will collect the list of queries that are executed within the track_queries block, and ask us to confirm that the list is correct.

```
$ bundle exec ruby -I test test/integration/query_test.rb
# Running:


@@ -1,0, +1,11 @@
+Thing Load
+Minion Load
+Minion Load
+Minion Load
+Minion Load
+Minion Load
+Minion Load
+Minion Load
+Minion Load
+Minion Load
+Minion Load
Accept the new value: yes to all, no to all, yes, no? [Y/N/y/n] (y):
```

Press y, and the test will update the assert_value call in the test/integration/query_test.rb file.

chp8/app/test/integration/query_test.rb
```
assert_value queries.join("\n"), <<-END
    Thing Load
    Minion Load
    Minion Load
    Minion Load
```

```
    Minion Load
    Minion Load
    Minion Load
    Minion Load
    Minion Load
    Minion Load
    Minion Load
END
```

As expected, this unoptimized code runs nine too many Minion Load queries.

Let's see how the optimized version performs. First, change the code inside the track_queries block:

chp8/app/test/integration/query_test.rb
```
queries = track_queries do
  get "/", preload: true
end
```

Next, run the test again and accept the new value.

```
$ bundle exec ruby -I test test/integration/query_test.rb
# Running:

@@ -1,11, +1,2 @@
Thing Load
Minion Load
-Minion Load
-Minion Load
-Minion Load
-Minion Load
-Minion Load
-Minion Load
-Minion Load
-Minion Load
-Minion Load
Accept the new value: yes to all, no to all, yes, no? [Y/N/y/n] (y): y
.

Finished in 21.327313s, 0.0469 runs/s, 0.0938 assertions/s.
1 runs, 2 assertions, 0 failures, 0 errors, 0 skips
```

The test will update the query assert to this:

chp8/app/test/integration/query_test.rb
```
assert_value queries.join("\n"), <<-END
    Thing Load
    Minion Load
END
```

Again as expected, the optimized version runs only two queries to load all our objects.

After optimization you can use this test as a reference. It will fail every time you introduce an additional query. At that point you'll either accept the change or reject it and fix your code.

Takeaways

Testing is the best way to maintain application performance after optimization. Let's summarize what it takes to do that.

1. Write performance tests—special kinds of integration tests that benchmark your code, keep results, and then assert performance by comparing current and previous benchmarks.

2. Make sure your performance tests get the measurements and comparisons right. Use the framework we wrote in this chapter to create your own performance tests.

3. When performance testing Rails, don't forget about database performance. Make sure you create enough data for performance tests, and check how many queries your requests run.

Congratulations! Now you know everything you need to know to optimize your Ruby code, measure optimization result, and ensure that your optimization persists.

But our quest for faster Ruby applications is not over yet. To optimize, we thought of our code as of a white box that we can dissect and improve. As you might guess, another approach would be to think of it as of a black box, and optimize the way we run the code by speeding up its dependencies and the whole execution environment. So let's do just that.

## CHAPTER 9

Think Outside the Box

Our ability to focus, as software engineers, makes us vulnerable to the tunnel vision syndrome. What that means when it comes to optimization is that when our Ruby program is slow, we tend to concentrate only on Ruby code optimization. But there are other ways to make our Ruby program faster, often resulting in a greater improvement than the obvious approach of looking for ways to optimize that Ruby code.

To find these other ways we have to step out of the box and look at how our program runs in the real world, what other software it uses, and where it's deployed. Our program will become faster if we find a better way to run it by optimizing all its dependencies and deployment infrastructure.

How exactly do we do that? I'll show you a couple of examples here in this chapter. But, unlike in the rest of my book, I can neither give you a complete solution nor outline the steps to be taken. There are simply too many ways to run the Ruby code, too many external tools it may use, and too many deployment platforms. So look at the material in this chapter as a source of inspiration for your own thinking outside the box, not as a complete guide.

Cycle Long-Running Instances

Let's first look at how our program runs, and decide what we can do to make it run faster.

Imagine you started a program. Let's say it's a web browser, and after some time it's become slow. What do you do? It's not a trick question. You know what you should do: restart it, and it'll be fast again.

Can we apply the same principle with Ruby programs? It turns out we can. Any long-running Ruby application will become faster after the restart.

Back in *Profile Memory* we talked about how garbage collector performance declines when the amount of memory allocated by the Ruby process increases. Spoiler alert: I'm going to jump ahead of myself and add to this one more fact. In most cases the Ruby process will never give the memory allocated for Ruby objects back to the operating system. Take a peek at the next chapter if you're curious what happens, and why.

For now, let's concentrate only on these two facts: (a) the performance declines with the increased memory usage, and (b) the amount of memory allocated by the Ruby process only grows with time.

What does this add up to? Slowdown. The longer our Ruby program runs, the slower it gets. No amount of code optimization can prevent this. Only a restart solves this slowdown!

So if you have a long-running Ruby instance, you'll need to cycle it. And by cycling I mean restarting it when it uses too much memory.

You can cycle Ruby applications in several ways:

- Use a hosting platform that does it for you. For example, Heroku cycles its "dynos" daily[1] and also aborts the process when it exceeds the dyno's memory limit.

- Use a process management tool, like monit,[2] god,[3] upstart,[4] runit,[5] or foreman with systemd.[6]

- Ask the operating system to kill your application if it exceeds the memory limit. Note that this still depends on a process management tool to restart the application after it gets killed.

If you deploy on Heroku, its daily cycling might work well for you. But when I worked on Acunote, we had our own deployment infrastructure and dedicated servers. So we had to use the other techniques to combat excessive memory usage. I'll show a few examples of how we did it.

---

1. https://devcenter.heroku.com/articles/how-heroku-works#dyno-manager
2. http://mmonit.com/monit/
3. http://godrb.com/
4. http://blog.arkency.com/2014/06/create-run-and-manage-your-background-processes-with-upstart/
5. http://smarden.org/runit/index.html and http://jtimberman.housepub.org/blog/2012/12/29/process-supervision-solved-problem/
6. http://ddollar.github.io/foreman/ and http://patrakov.blogspot.com/2011/01/writing-systemd-service-files.html

Example: Configure Monit to Cycle Ruby Processes

With monit we can check totalmem and loadavg variables and restart based on their values, like this:

```
check process my_ruby_process
  with pidfile /var/run/my_ruby_process/my_ruby_process.pid
  start program = "my_ruby_process start"
  stop program = "my_ruby_process stop"
  # eating up memory?
  if totalmem is greater than 300.0 MB for 3 cycles then restart
  # bad, bad, bad
  if loadavg(5min) greater than 10 for 8 cycles then restart
  # something is wrong, call the sys-admin
  if 20 restarts within 20 cycles then timeout
```

Example: Set Operating System Memory Limit

On Unix systems we can use the setrlimit system call to enforce the process memory limit.

For example, on Linux and Mac OS X, set RLIMIT_AS:

```
# 600 MB RSS limit
Process.setrlimit(Process::RLIMIT_AS, 600 * 1024 * 1024)
```

Example: Cycle Unicorn Workers in the Rails Application

Rails applications running on the Unicorn web server can cycle themselves without any external process management tool. The idea is to set a memory limit for workers and let the master process restart them once they get killed.

For example, this is what I have in my config/unicorn.rb:

```
after_fork do |server, worker|
  worker.set_memory_limits
end

class Unicorn::Worker
  MEMORY_LIMIT = 600 #MB

  def set_memory_limits
    Process.setrlimit(Process::RLIMIT_AS, MEMORY_LIMIT * 1024 * 1024)
  end
end
```

That works for Unicorn 4.4, so you might need to change it to work with newer versions.

> ### Joe asks:
> ## How Large Should My Memory Limit Be?
>
> Modern Rails applications take from 100 MB to 200 MB after startup. So I wouldn't set this limit lower than 250 MB. And you probably want to go higher. How high? To get a good approximation, take the amount of memory available to Rails and divide by the number of Unicorn workers.

The only problem with this approach is that the operating system may kill your worker while serving the request. To avoid that, I also set up what I call the *kind* memory limit.

We can set this limit to a value lower than the RSS memory limit, and check for it after every request. Once the worker reaches the kind memory limit, it gracefully shuts itself down.

This way, in most cases workers quit before reaching the RSS memory limit enforced by the operating system. That becomes a safeguard only against long-running requests that grow too big in memory.

Here's how I set up the kind limit with Unicorn:

```ruby
class Unicorn::HttpServer
  KIND_MEMORY_LIMIT = 250 #MB

  alias process_client_orig process_client
  undef_method :process_client
  def process_client(client)
    process_client_orig(client)
    exit if get_memory_size(Process.pid) > KIND_MEMORY_LIMIT
  end

  def get_memory_size(pid)
    status = File.read("/proc/#{pid}/status")
    matches = status.match(/VmRSS:\s+(\d+)/)
    matches[1].to_i / 1024
  end
end
```

This example will work only for Linux and other Unixes because it gets the current process memory usage from the /proc filesystem. If you'd like to port it for Mac OS or Windows, you'll have to rewrite the get_memory_size function.

There are, of course, many other ways to keep the Ruby process from growing in memory. I can't describe all of them in this book, but by now you should have the general idea. Whatever tool you use, make sure it restarts the long-running Ruby application before it grows too big in memory.

Fork to Run Heavy Jobs

Cycling long-running Ruby instances helps to deal with sudden increases in memory consumption. But often we know beforehand that the code we're going to execute will need memory. For example, our database query returned 100,000 rows, and we need to compute complex statistics based on that data.

We can let that memory-heavy operation run and then let our infrastructure restart the Ruby process. But there's a better solution. We can fork our process and execute the memory-heavy code in the child process. This way, only the child process will grow in memory, and when it exits, the parent process remains unaffected.

The simplest possible implementation looks like this:

```
pid = fork do
  heavy_function
end
Process::waitpid(pid)
```

You might recognize this code from the performance_benchmark function in the previous chapter. We used the same fork-and-run approach to isolate benchmarks from the parent process, and from themselves.

You might also recall the downside of this approach. Such code has no easy way of returning data to the parent process. If you want to do it, you'll need to open a pipe between parent and child, use temporary storage, or store results into the database.

In the previous chapter we already used the temporary storage to communicate between the forked process and its parent. So now let's see how to send the data via the I/O pipe.

```
chp9/forked_process_io_pipe_example.rb
require 'bigdecimal'

def heavy_function
  # this allocates approx. 450,000 extra objects before returning the result
  Array.new(100000) { BigDecimal(rand(), 3) }.inject(0) { |sum, i| sum + i }
end

# disable GC to compute object allocation statistics
GC.disable
puts "Total Ruby objects before operation: #{ObjectSpace.count_objects[:TOTAL]}"
```

```ruby
# open pipe, then close "read" end on child side,
# and "write" end on parent side
read, write = IO.pipe

pid = fork do
  # child may run GC as usual
  GC.enable

  read.close
  result = heavy_function
  # use Marshal.dump to save Ruby objects into the pipe
  Marshal.dump(result, write)

  exit!(0)
end

write.close
result = read.read
# make sure we wait until the child finishes
Process.wait(pid)

# use Marshal.dump to load Ruby objects from pipe
puts Marshal.load(result).inspect

# this number should be not too different from the previous one
puts "Total Ruby objects after operation: #{ObjectSpace.count_objects[:TOTAL]}"
```

When we run the code, we see that despite the child allocating 400,000–450,000 objects, the parent process doesn't grow at all.

```
$ ruby forked_process_io_pipe_example.rb
Total Ruby objects before operation: 30163
#<BigDecimal:7f99b3a612e8,'0.5016076916 4137E5',18(27)>
Total Ruby objects after operation: 30163
```

This technique is very useful for long-running Ruby applications that occasionally have to perform memory-heavy operations. But for Rails, there are usually better solutions.

Most modern deployments support the idea of background jobs. For example, delayed_job gem[7] essentially implements the same idea. It lets you delay any function call by serializing the function and its data into the database, and then executing the code in the separated, short-lived process (usually launched by a rake task).

There are many other background job implementations that do the same thing. You can use any of them.

---

7.   https://github.com/collectiveidea/delayed_job

But beware of the ones that use threads instead of separate processes. A notable example is Sidekiq.[8] It is usually one Ruby process running several dozen Ruby threads. All these share the same ObjectSpace, so when one thread grows, the whole process needs a restart. So make sure you use one of the process management tools we talked about earlier to monitor and restart the Sidekiq worker.

Both cycling and forking keep the Ruby process under a certain memory limit, so that GC has less work to do and takes less time to complete. It's GC time that we're really optimizing here.

Do Out-of-Band Garbage Collection

Despite all our optimization efforts, GC will continue to take a substantial part of execution time. So what do we do if we can't reduce GC time? We force GC when our application isn't doing anything. That approach is called Out-of-Band Garbage Collection (OOBGC).

No OOBGC Necessary for Ruby Version 2.2 and Higher

Why is it important to reduce GC time or do GC while your code is idle? Because your application must stop and wait for (the marking phase of) GC to finish. However, with Ruby 2.2 and its incremental GC, the "stop the world" time is much less than before. So chances are you'll never need OOBGC if you use Ruby 2.2 and later. You'll see why in the next chapter.

Idle time is something that we usually observe in web applications and services. So let me show you how to configure OOBGC for the most popular Ruby web servers.

Example: OOBGC with Unicorn

Unicorn[9] has direct support for OOBGC.

If you use Ruby 2.1 or later, add the gctools gem[10] to your Gemfile and put this into your config.ru for Unicorn:

```
require 'gctools/oobgc'
use(GC::OOB::UnicornMiddleware)
```

---

8.   http://sidekiq.org/
9.   http://unicorn.bogomips.org/
10. https://github.com/tmm1/gctools

When does the OOBGC happen? You might guess it should run after every N requests. But that would add unnecessary load to your server. Not all requests are the same, and some of them might leave little to no garbage.

The gctools library does it in a better way. Ruby 2.1 exposes enough information about its internal state for the gctools to decide when the collection is required. You can read more about how it works, and what results to expect, in its author's blog.[11]

However, if you're still using Ruby version 2.0 and lower, then the only OOBGC strategy is to force GC after every N requests. Unicorn has the built-in middleware for that:

```
require 'unicorn/oob_gc'
use(Unicorn::OobGC, 1)
```

Here the second parameter to the use() call is the frequency of OOBGC: 1 means after every request, 2 means after every two requests, and so on.

Example: OOBGC in Other Web Servers or Applications

We can use the gctools library to do OOBGC in any code. Once we determine when our code has idle time, we can call this:

```
require 'gctools/oobgc'
GC::OOB.run
```

There are two things to keep in mind when implementing OOBGC on your own.

First, make sure that you get your OOBGC timing right. For web applications, it's after the request body is flushed into the stream. For background workers, it's after finishing the task and before pulling the next task from the queue.

Second, be careful if you use threads. If you force GC from one thread while the other is still doing its job, you will block that other thread. So you should make sure all threads in the process are doing nothing before calling OOBGC.

That's why, for example, the Puma web server doesn't support OOBGC. Unlike Unicorn, Puma's workers can be multithreaded, and there's no single point in time when you can safely perform OOBGC.

---

11. http://tmm1.net/ruby21-oobgc

Tune Your Database

Your database server can be either a liability or an asset to performance. If you use one of the modern SQL databases, don't treat it as a dumb storage mechanism. We have seen in *Offload Work to the Database*, on page 34 how rewriting Ruby code into SQL can give you one or more orders of magnitude improvement.

But equally important is having your database server tuned up for optimal performance. You'll want to do this, because the default settings are usually inadequate, especially for PostgreSQL.

Example: Tune Up PostgreSQL for Optimal Performance

This example is relevant for you only when you have to set up the database server on your own. If you host on Heroku, then you can expect your PostgreSQL to be configured reasonably well. That might be true for other hosting solutions.

PostgreSQL has a plethora of configuration options, so instead of diving into details, we'll talk at a high level about what we need to configure.

- Let the database use as much memory as possible. Ideally, all your data should fit into RAM for faster access.

- Make sure the database has enough memory to store intermediate results, especially for sorts and aggregations.

- Set the database to log slow queries and preserve as much information about them as possible to reproduce the problem.

Let me show you the PostgreSQL configuration snippet that implements these goals. This is an extract from the config we used for Acunote. It's not a complete config, so you should review these settings, read comments, and merge with your own config as necessary.

```
chp9/postgresql.conf
# For all memory settings below, RAM_FOR_DATABASE is the amount of memory
# available to the PostgreSQL after the operating system and all other
# services are started.
#
# Evaluate the Ruby pseudocode in angle brackets and replace
# it with actual values.


# ============================================================================
# Use as Much Memory as Possible
# ============================================================================
```

```
# How much memory we have for database disk caches in memory
# Note, disk caching is controlled by the operating system,
# so this setting is just a guideline.
# Recommended setting: RAM_FOR_DATABASE * 3/4
set effective_cache_size <ram_for_database.to_i * 3/4>MB

# Shared memory that PostgreSQL itself allocates for data caching in RAM
# Recommended setting: RAM_FOR_DATABASE/4
# Warning: on Linux make sure to increase the SHMMAX kernel setting.
set shared_buffers <ram_for_database.to_i / 4>MB


# ============================================================================
# Allocate Enough Memory for Intermediate Results
# ============================================================================

# Work memory for queries (to store sort results, aggregates, etc.)
# This is a per-connection setting, so it depends on the expected
# maximum number of active connections.
# Recommended setting: (RAM_FOR_DATABASE/max_connections) ROUND DOWN 2^x
set work_mem < 2**(Math.log(ram_for_database.to_i /
  expected_max_active_connections.to_i)/Math.log(2)).floor >MB

# Memory for vacuum, autovacuum, index creation
# Recommended setting: RAM_FOR_DATABASE/16 ROUND DOWN 2^x
set maintenance_work_mem < 2**(Math.log(ram_for_database.to_i / 16)
  /Math.log(2)).floor >MB


# ============================================================================
# Log Slow Queries
# ============================================================================

# Log only autovacuum's longer than 1 sec.
set log_autovacuum_min_duration 1000ms

# Log long queries.
set log_min_duration_statement 1000ms
set auto_explain.log_min_duration 1000ms

# Explain long queries in the log using the auto_explain plug-in.
set shared_preload_libraries 'auto_explain'
set custom_variable_classes 'auto_explain'

# But do not use explain analyze, which may be slow
set auto_explain.log_analyze off
```

You might have noticed that this configuration mostly optimizes PostgreSQL memory usage. Yes, it's memory again. We spent the greater part of this book talking about Ruby memory optimization, and now it's our database that also needs memory tuning.

That's not a coincidence. Modern software is rarely limited by CPU. The most severe limitation is the amount of available memory, followed by network latency and throughput, and disk I/O.

That's why, no matter what database you use, you need to make sure it has and uses as much memory as possible.

Buy Enough Resources for Production

A large number of Ruby applications run in the cloud today. There are many providers of deployment infrastructure, but the better ones tend to be expensive. So you often have to find the optimal compromise between the price you pay and the resource limits you get for that price.

Hosting providers usually emphasize the number of CPU cores and the size of the storage in their pricing plans. Both these numbers are irrelevant. CPU performance is usually not a problem, and storage can be easily added. Here are what I believe are the most important criteria when evaluating the potential deployment stack:

1. Total RAM available.

   After reading this book, it should be no surprise that memory comes first in my list.

2. I/O performance.

   This is the most overlooked parameter, which is often hard to evaluate without deploying at least the test application. It doesn't matter for some applications, but if you write logs or cache to disk, pay attention to it.

3. Database configuration.

   If you do not set up the database server yourself, make sure your provider follows the best practices that we talked about earlier.

4. Everything else.

Don't be afraid to pay for more memory. That is often cheaper than paying for extra servers (virtual machines). For example, as of this writing, Heroku, one of the most popular Rails deployment solutions, offers two kinds of dynos (virtual machines): 1X and 2X. The first has 512 MB of RAM, and the second has 1024 MB. 2X is about 2–2.5 times more expensive.

On the 1X dyno you can run only one Rails instance because their average size is about 250–300 MB. On the 2X dyno you can run three instances—for example, three Unicorn workers. That more than justifies the increase in cost.

Also, when your Rails application goes bad and grows in memory, you'll at least have some extra memory on a 2X dyno to be used before you cycle the offending process. In my experience that makes all the difference. With a 1X dyno your application can just stop responding whereas 2X will slow down for a short time.

I/O bit me several times in the past. At Acunote, we used to deploy on Engine Yard before we bought our own hardware. Their virtual machines at the time did not have their own storage, and instead used the network filesystem (RedHat GFS).

GFS seemed to work really well for us until I found that certain cache expiration calls took too long to execute.

We cached to disk, and expired it by traversing the whole cache directory and matching the file paths to the expiration regular expression. It turned out that GFS had a slow fstat() implementation, so traversing the large cache directory could take several seconds. So we had to change our caching strategy to limit the number of directories in the search path for expiration.

Takeaways

When optimizing your application, look beyond the code in your search for performance problems. Sometimes an unoptimized application running on a properly configured software stack will perform better than the thoroughly optimized one in a poorly configured stack.

This chapter has expored several items you need to think about when deploying your Ruby application:

- Restart your long-running processes when they grow too large in memory. A freshly started application runs faster because the GC has fewer objects to collect.

- Run heavy tasks in an isolated forked environment. This way the forked process will give back to the operating system all the memory allocated during its execution.

- Do out-of-band garbage collection if you use Ruby version 2.0 and lower, and your application has idle time. This reduces GC stop-the-world time when your code is actually doing its job.

- Tune up your database and any other software for optimal performance. Popular PostgreSQL database has over-conservative defaults that are harmful for performance.

- Review your deployment stack and identify possible sources of slowdowns. If in doubt what to improve in your infrastructure first, buy more memory.

Remember, this list is not exhaustive. Take it as a hint, a starting point, rather than official advice. Forget your Ruby code for a moment, and take a fresh look at how and where it runs. You'll be surprised by the slowdowns you'll find.

So we've talked about tuning your Ruby program and the software it uses for optimal performance. But so far we've ignored the elephant in the room. The Ruby interpreter itself is the most important piece of software that your program runs on. And it needs performance tuning too. That's what we'll talk about in the next chapter.

## CHAPTER 10

Tune Up the Garbage Collector

Many of the optimizations so far in this book involved avoiding or postponing GC as much as possible. But we can only do so much by working around the GC's inefficiency. Let's instead look into the face of evil. Ruby GC is, in fact, not a black box. We can understand it. And with modern Ruby interpreters, we can control it. This means that we can tune up GC for optimal performance in our applications.

That is, of course, only possible if we know enough about Ruby and GC internals. So let's first figure out how they work, and then talk about tuning the GC settings.

Understand How Ruby Uses Memory

Ruby stores objects in its own heap, and uses operating system heap for data that doesn't fit into objects. Let's see how that works.

Objects

In Ruby everything is an object that's internally represented as the RVALUE struct. sizeof(RVALUE) is machine dependent:

- 20 bytes in 32-bit architecture when double is 4-byte aligned

- 24 bytes in 32-bit architecture when double is 8-byte aligned

- 40 bytes in 64-bit architecture

Most modern computers are 64-bit, so we'll assume that one object costs us 40 bytes of memory to create.

You can see the object size on your computer in the debugger. I'm running my examples on 64-bit Linux, so I'll use the gdb debugger. If you are on Mac OS X, try lldb that comes with the Xcode command-line tools. It's compatible with gdb, and examples from this book should run without modification. On Windows, the easiest way is to install MinGW,[1] which includes the gdb debugger.

This is how you can get the object size in the debugger:

```
$ gdb `rbenv which ruby`
(gdb) p sizeof(RVALUE)
$1 = 40
(gdb)
```

As expected, it's 40 bytes on my 64-bit Linux system.

Note that gdb requires the argument to be an executable and not a shell wrapper, for example, the one that rbenv installs. That's why I call rbenv which to get the actual path to the Ruby executable and pass it to the debugger.

Is 40 bytes per object a large overhead? It doesn't sound like a lot, but numbers will add up quickly at runtime.

A medium-sized Rails application will allocate half a million objects at startup. That translates to about 20 MB of memory just to store the objects. And this estimate doesn't include extra space that you might need to store objects' data.

In addition to that, to save time during object creation, Ruby preallocates extra space and thus uses even more memory than necessary to keep all existing objects. Let's see how.

Ruby Objects Heap

Ruby allocates objects in the heap space that consists of heap pages. Each heap page in turn is divided into slots, one slot for one object.

When Ruby wants to allocate an object, it takes up the unused slot from the heap. If there are not enough free slots, Ruby grows the heap space by adding one or more heap pages. How much is added depends on the current heap usage, interpreter version, and the heap growth algorithm parameters.

Ruby 1.8

Ruby 1.8 adds one heap page at a time. The first page that is created at startup contains HEAP_MIN_SLOTS slots. This constant is defined in gc.c and is equal to 10000 by default.

---

1.   http://www.mingw.org/

Subsequent pages will be larger by a factor of 1.8. For example, the second page will have 18,000 slots; the third, 32,400; and so on. The total number of slots will be 10,000, 28,000, 60,400, and so on.

Ruby 1.9 and 2.0

Ruby 1.9 and later use a slightly different heap growth algorithm. First, the heap growth factor defines the growth of the whole heap space, not the individual heap page as in 1.8. Second, instead of adding one ever-increasing heap page at a time, it preallocates several fixed-sized heap pages.

Smaller heap pages theoretically help to reduce memory fragmentation and make it easier to reclaim unused heap space. We'll explore later in this chapter how well that theory corresponds to real life.

Each heap page in Ruby >= 1.9 is 16 kB (minus extra several dozen bytes required for upkeep); 16 kB is enough to keep, for example, 408 objects on a 64-bit Linux system. The HEAP_OBJ_LIMIT constant tells us the number of objects in a heap page:

```
$ gdb `rbenv which ruby`
(gdb) p HEAP_OBJ_LIMIT*1
$1 = 408
(gdb)
```

Let's investigate how object preallocation works. First, we'll talk about Ruby 1.9, the simplest of modern implementations.

At startup, Ruby 1.9 preallocates HEAP_MIN_SLOTS / HEAP_OBJ_LIMIT heap pages. With default settings, it's 10,000 / 408 = 24 heap pages on my system.

When the interpreter needs to add more heap space, it takes the number of pages currently used, multiplies that by a factor of 1.8, and allocates the missing heap pages.

For example, once those 24 heaps created at startup are taken, Ruby grows the heap space to 24 * 1.8 = 43, adding (43 - 24) = 19 new heaps. These 43 heaps will have space for 43 * HEAP_OBJ_LIMIT = 43 * 408 = 17,544 object slots. Next time the heap grows to 43 * 1.8 = 77 heaps, giving us 77 * 408 = 31,416 slots.

Note that with this algorithm, heap growth is much slower than in 1.8, thus reducing total memory usage in applications.

You can see the heap growth for yourself with GC#stat in irb.

```
$ rbenv shell 1.9.3-p551
$ irb
```

```
irb(main):001:0> require 'pp'
=> true
irb(main):002:0> pp GC.stat; nil
{:count=>7,
 :heap_used=>77,
 :heap_length=>77,
 :heap_increment=>0,
 :heap_live_num=>14208,
 :heap_free_num=>17146,
 :heap_final_num=>104}
=> nil
```

Let me explain the numbers that GC#stat returns:

count

>The number of times GC ran.

heap_used

>The number of heap pages allocated.

>The larger this number is, the more memory our Ruby process consumes, and the more work GC has to do.

>To estimate the Ruby heap memory consumption, multiply this by HEAP_OBJ_LIMIT and sizeof(RVALUE).

>In our example, the memory used for heap is 77 * 408 * 40 = 1,256,640 bytes, about 1.2 MB.

>The name of this parameter is misleading. It doesn't necessarily mean that all of these heap pages are used. They might be allocated, but empty. Also, this number isn't cumulative. It can be decreased if Ruby shrinks the heap space.

heap_increment

>In theory, this should be the number of heap pages that can be allocated before the interpreter needs to run the GC and grow the heap space again.

>In practice, this number is always 0 in Ruby 1.9.

heap_length

>The total number of heap pages, including heap_used and heap_increment.

heap_live_num

>The current number of live objects in the heap.

>This number includes objects that are still live but will be collected next time GC runs. So we can't use it to estimate the number of free slots in the heap.

heap_free_num

> The current number of free object slots in the heap after the last GC run.

> This number is also misleading and can't be used to estimate the current number of free slots. The only way to know how much free space you have on the heap is to call GC.start before looking at the heap_free_num.

heap_final_num

> The number of objects that weren't finalized during the last GC and that will be finalized later.

Now that we know what GC#stat's return values mean, let's get back to our irb session and try to make sense out of the numbers we see.

After startup, irb has 77 heap pages allocated. This means there were three growth iterations: one at interpreter startup (24 pages), and two more during irb initialization (giving us 43 and 77 pages in total).

We can predict that the next time the heap grows, it will increase to 77 * 1.8 = 138 pages.

To observe this in irb, we must know how many extra objects we need to allocate. So we'll force GC, and allocate slightly more than heap_free_num.

```
irb(main):003:0> GC.start
=> nil
irb(main):004:0> pp GC.stat; nil
{:count=>8,
 :heap_used=>77,
 :heap_length=>77,
 :heap_increment=>0,
 :heap_live_num=>12635,
 :heap_free_num=>18764,
 :heap_final_num=>0}
=> nil
irb(main):005:0> x = Array.new(19000) { Object.new }; nil
=> nil
irb(main):006:0> pp GC.stat; nil
{:count=>9,
 :heap_used=>138,
 :heap_length=>138,
 :heap_increment=>0,
 :heap_live_num=>30215,
 :heap_free_num=>26156,
 :heap_final_num=>42}
=> nil
```

Everything looks right. We have slightly fewer than 19,000 free slots on the heap. And when we allocate 19,000 objects, we observe the heap growth from 77 to 138 pages as predicted.

Ruby 2.1

Ruby 2.1 renames the HEAP_MIN_SLOTS constant to GC_HEAP_INIT_SLOTS and adds heap growth control. Instead of hard-coding 1.8, it defines the GC_HEAP_GROWTH_FACTOR constant. That still defaults to 1.8, though.

In addition we can set a cap on the heap growth. If we set the GC_HEAP_GROWTH_MAX_SLOTS constant, Ruby will add no more than the specified number of slots any time it grows the heap. This way we can force the heap growth to become linear at a certain point. We'll talk a bit later about how that can be useful.

While the growth factor is still the same 1.8 times, heap growth is more conservative in Ruby 2.1. To calculate the heap pages increment, the interpreter takes only the number of allocated, nonempty slots, and multiplies that by the growth factor.

If we try to observe the growth effect in Ruby 2.1, we see that the heap length numbers are a bit off. For example, this is what I see when I run irb in Ruby 2.1.5:

```
$ rbenv shell 2.1.5
$ irb

irb(main):001:0> GC.stat[:heap_length]
=> 81
```

Why is the heap length 81 instead of 77 as in the similar Ruby 1.9 example earlier? It's because Ruby 2.1 creates one heap page at startup before allocating the initial 24 pages. This way we get 25 pages, which then grow to 25 * 1.8 = 45, and then to 45 * 1.8 = 81.

GC#stat in Ruby 2.1 returns more information:

```
$ rbenv shell 2.1.5
$ irb

irb(main):001:0> require 'pp'
=> true
irb(main):002:0> pp GC.stat; nil
{:count=>7,
 :heap_used=>81,
 :heap_length=>81,
 :heap_increment=>0,
 :heap_live_slot=>32505,
```

```
    :heap_free_slot=>501,
    :heap_final_slot=>0,
    :heap_swept_slot=>19441,
    :heap_eden_page_length=>81,
    :heap_tomb_page_length=>0,
    :total_allocated_object=>93148,
    :total_freed_object=>60643,
    :malloc_increase=>322184,
    :malloc_limit=>16777216,
    :minor_gc_count=>5,
    :major_gc_count=>2,
    :remembered_shady_object=>195,
    :remembered_shady_object_limit=>300,
    :old_object=>10585,
    :old_object_limit=>11680,
    :oldmalloc_increase=>2470360,
    :oldmalloc_limit=>16777216}
=> nil
```

Here are some of the parameters that are relevant to heap allocation:

count, heap_used, heap_length, heap_increment
Same as in Ruby 1.9, except that heap_increment is not always zero anymore.

The heap space in Ruby 2.1 and later grows gradually. When Ruby grows the heap space, it only allocates the space in the list of heap pages. heap_length tells you the length of that list. Actual pages are allocated on demand. heap_used shows how many of them are allocated at any given time. heap_increment shows how many pages can be allocated.

This change means that newer Ruby interpreters grow the heap space gradually, without the spikes in memory usage.

heap_live_slot, heap_free_slot, heap_final_slot
Same as heap_live_num, heap_free_num, and heap_final_num in Ruby 1.9.

One important difference is that heap_free_num refers to the number of free slots in the allocated heap pages. So to estimate the free space in the heap, add the number of slots that can be allocated in the heap, like this: heap_increment * HEAP_OBJ_LIMIT + heap_free_num.

heap_swept_slot
The number of slots swept (freed) during the last GC.

total_allocated_object, total_freed_object
The number of allocated and freed objects during the process lifetime.

heap_eden_page_length, heap_tomb_page_length
The number of heap pages in eden and tomb.

The heap space in Ruby 2.1 and later is divided into *eden* and *tomb*. This is the Ruby way to keep track of occupied and empty heap pages. The former are in the eden; the latter go into the tomb.

When allocating objects, Ruby looks for free space in the eden pages first. Only if there's no space in eden, it takes a free page from tomb. This algorithm is good for two reasons. First, it reduces memory fragmentation by reusing empty pages only as necessary. But second, and most important, it gives more opportunity to the interpreter to destroy them and free up unused heap space.

Let me explain why.

Ruby interpreters before 2.1 could not really shrink the heap space. Once allocated, the page was likely to stay there until the program exits. For example, in Ruby 1.8 each subsequent heap page is bigger than the previous one by a factor of 1.8. And the bigger the page is, the less likely it is to become empty and be a candidate for destruction. Even fixed-size pages in Ruby 1.9 are not that likely to be freed because of memory fragmentation.

So, theoretically, Ruby 2.1 should have a better chance of freeing up the heap space. Let's see if that works. First, we'll start irb and create 100,000 objects:

```
$ rbenv shell 2.1.5
$ irb

irb(main):001:0> GC.start
=> nil
irb(main):002:0> "eden: %d, tomb: %d" % [GC.stat[:heap_eden_page_length],
  GC.stat[:heap_tomb_page_length]]
=> "eden: 81, tomb: 0"
irb(main):003:0> x = Array.new(100000) { Object.new }; nil
=> nil
irb(main):004:0> "eden: %d, tomb: %d" % [GC.stat[:heap_eden_page_length],
  GC.stat[:heap_tomb_page_length]]
=> "eden: 277, tomb: 0"
```

So far, all pages are on the eden because they contain live objects. Now let's clear the reference to our array of objects and call GC to free it up:

```
irb(main):005:0> x = nil
=> nil
irb(main):006:0> GC.start
=> nil
irb(main):007:0> "eden: %d, tomb: %d" % [GC.stat[:heap_eden_page_length],
  GC.stat[:heap_tomb_page_length]]
=> "eden: 84, tomb: 168"
```

Your numbers might be a bit different, but you should see the same pattern. From 277 eden pages, 84 remained used. That's almost the same number of pages (81) as before we created our 100,000 objects.

A total of 168 pages became empty and got into the tomb. The rest, 277 – 84 – 168 = 25 pages were freed up. If we translate that into bytes, we'll see that Ruby freed up 400 kB (25 pages) out of 4.3 MB (277 pages), reducing the heap size by about 9%. This reduction is not significant, but it indeed happens.

Why did Ruby decide to keep 168 unused pages in the heap? It's because it doesn't want to shrink heap space too much. The interpreter makes an assumption that if you created a lot of objects before, you'll tend to continue creating a lot of objects in the future. That's not always true, but I can't say the assumption is unreasonable.

This is the algorithm that Ruby uses to determine the number of heap pages to free.

1. Take the number of pages swept during GC, meaning pages where GC found at least one object to collect.

   In our case we dereferenced 100,000 objects, so GC had to sweep about 100,000 / HEAP_OBJ_LIMIT = 245 pages.

2. Calculate the maximum number of slots that should stay in the heap. This number is either 80% of total heap slot count or GC_HEAP_INIT_SLOTS, whichever is bigger.

   In our case it's 80% of 277 = 221 pages.

3. The number of pages to be freed is the difference between these two numbers. If the difference is negative, then no pages will be freed.

   In our case the number of pages to free is 245 – 221 = 24. In reality Ruby freed up 25 pages, mostly because GC had more pages to sweep due to fragmentation.

As you see, the heap space can indeed shrink in Ruby 2.1, but by not too much. Ten percent is about the maximum reduction you'll ever see. This is certainly not enough to prevent your Ruby process from growing over time because, by default, growth is 80% while reduction is only 10%.

So in production just assume that your Ruby process will always grow, and be sure to periodically restart the long-running processes as we discussed back in *Cycle Long-Running Instances*, on page 135.

Ruby 2.2

Ruby 2.2 changes GC#stat parameters yet again, and introduces some new ones. Let's review them:

```
$ rbenv shell 2.2.0
$ irb
```

```
irb(main):001:0> require 'pp'
=> true
irb(main):002:0> pp GC.stat
{:count=>7,
 :heap_allocated_pages=>74,
 :heap_sorted_length=>75,
 :heap_allocatable_pages=>0,
 :heap_available_slots=>30160,
 :heap_live_slots=>29620,
 :heap_free_slots=>540,
 :heap_final_slots=>0,
 :heap_marked_slots=>11631,
 :heap_swept_slots=>10126,
 :heap_eden_pages=>74,
 :heap_tomb_pages=>0,
 :total_allocated_pages=>74,
 :total_freed_pages=>0,
 :total_allocated_objects=>90529,
 :total_freed_objects=>60909,
 :malloc_increase_bytes=>212728,
 :malloc_increase_bytes_limit=>16777216,
 :minor_gc_count=>5,
 :major_gc_count=>2,
 :remembered_wb_unprotected_objects=>180,
 :remembered_wb_unprotected_objects_limit=>278,
 :old_objects=>10922,
 :old_objects_limit=>11004,
 :oldmalloc_increase_bytes=>1503376,
 :oldmalloc_increase_bytes_limit=>16777216}
```

Let's again ignore malloc parameters, and look only at those relevant to heap space:

heap_allocated_pages, heap_allocatable_pages, heap_sorted_pages
> These are the heap_used, heap_increment, and heap_length variables that we know from Ruby 2.1.

heap_live_slots, heap_free_slots, heap_final_slots
> Same as heap_live_num, heap_free_num, heap_final_num in Ruby 2.1.

heap_available_slots
> The number of all available slots: heap_live_slots + heap_free_slots + heap_final_slots.

heap_marked_slots, heap_swept_slots

  The number of slots marked and swept during the last GC.

heap_eden_pages, heap_tomb_pages

  Same as heap_eden_page_length and heap_tomb_page_length.

total_allocated_pages, total_freed_pages, total_allocated_objects, total_freed_objects

  In addition to the total cumulative numbers of allocated and freed objects, Ruby 2.2 lets us know the total number of allocated and freed pages during the interpreter's lifetime.

Ruby 2.2 takes an even more conservative approach to growing the heap space than 2.1. Before, the growth was relative to the number of allocated pages (heap_used or heap_allocated_pages. Starting from 2.2, the growth is relative to the number of eden pages (heap_eden_pages). That number may be smaller, because allocated pages may go into the tomb if unused.

You can see this for yourself in irb, similarly to how we did it earlier for Ruby 1.9 and 2.1. Don't worry if the page and slot numbers are not exactly what you think they should be. Ruby can reuse object slots and free or resurrect heaps. That complicates calculations. Just make sure you understand the big picture.

Now you know how memory is allocated and used for Ruby objects. By looking at GC#stat parameters you can find out how much memory is needed, how much can be allocated without doing GC, and what will happen to the object space after GC. This is necessary to know when you are stuck with high memory usage, and want to understand what happens.

But that's not the whole story about memory usage. Remember, a Ruby object is 40 bytes at maximum. What if the data you're storing into memory is larger than 40 bytes—for example, a large string that you've read from a file?

In Ruby that extra data doesn't belong in the heap space, and is allocated and managed separately. Let's see where and how.

Object Memory

A Ruby object can store only a limited amount of data, up to 40 bytes in a 64-bit system. Slightly less than half of that is required for upkeep. All data that does not fit into the object itself is dynamically allocated outside of the Ruby heap. When the object is swept by GC, the memory is freed.

For example, a Ruby string stores only 23 bytes in the RSTRING object on a 64-bit system. When the string length becomes larger than 23 bytes, Ruby allo-

cates additional memory for it. We can see how much by calling
ObjectSpace#memsize_of, for example, like this:

```
$ rbenv shell 2.2.0
$ irb

irb(main):001:0> require 'objspace'
=> true
irb(main):002:0> str = 'x'
=> "x"
irb(main):003:0> ObjectSpace.memsize_of(str)
=> 40
irb(main):004:0> str = 'x'*23
=> "xxxxxxxxxxxxxxxxxxxxxxx"
irb(main):005:0> ObjectSpace.memsize_of(str)
=> 40
irb(main):006:0> str = 'x'*24
=> "xxxxxxxxxxxxxxxxxxxxxxxx"
irb(main):007:0> ObjectSpace.memsize_of(str)
=> 65
```

In this example we first create a string with one character. It fits into the
Ruby object, so ObjectSpace#memsize_of reports that 40 bytes is used. If we run
the same example in Ruby 2.1, we'll see 0 in the output. That's because older
interpreters do not include the size of the Ruby object itself into the number
returned by ObjectSpace#memsize_of.

When the string is more than 23 bytes, it's stored outside the object. The total
size of the large string is 65 bytes: 40 for the Ruby object on the heap, 24
bytes dynamically allocated outside of the heap to store the whole string, and
1 byte for upkeep.

Files, long arrays, large hashes, and others get extra memory in the same
way.

Unlike the heap space, Ruby allocates this additional object memory only on
demand, and frees it up when the object is finalized.

So, if our program creates a large string and then discards its contents, the
memory goes back to the operating system right away. Let's see for ourselves:

```
chp10/additional_object_memory.rb
puts "memory usage at start %d MB" %
  (`ps -o rss= -p #{Process.pid}`.to_i/1024)

str = "x" * 1024 * 1024 * 10  # 10 MB

puts "memory usage after large string creation %d MB" %
  (`ps -o rss= -p #{Process.pid}`.to_i/1024)
```

```
str = nil
GC.start(full_mark: true, immediate_sweep: true)

puts "memory usage after string is finalized %d MB" %
  (`ps -o rss= -p #{Process.pid}`.to_i/1024)
```

$ ruby additional_object_memory.rb
```
memory usage at start 8 MB
memory usage after large string creation 19 MB
memory usage after string is finalized 8 MB
```

Because this memory is allocated outside the heap space, it has almost no effect on garbage collection time. So it may be actually OK to allocate large amounts of data in memory if it ends up in the extra memory of one object.

For example, after reading the large file we'll get one big string object in memory. When we're done with the file contents, the memory it used goes back to the operating system. But if we parse the file, we might create a large number of Ruby objects, increasing the heap size and total memory usage more or less permanently.

That said, the very fact that we allocate extra memory might trigger GC. So yes, by allocating one big object we won't be adding work for GC, but we might be increasing the number of collections required. There's no free lunch in Ruby.

Now that you how Ruby allocates memory, you can understand what exactly GC is doing for us. Ruby can run without any GC, but it'd take too much memory. So the only task GC has to do is keep the memory usage of the Ruby process within reasonable limits. Let's see how that works.

Know What Triggers GC

As you now know, GC must control both the object allocation in the heap space and the object memory allocation outside the Ruby heap. Consequently, two events will trigger GC:

- There are not enough free slots in the heap space.

- The current memory allocation (malloc) limit has been exceeded.

So any object creation or memory allocation can invoke GC. Let's see when that happens, and then talk about how we can reduce the number of GC runs.

GC Triggered by Heap Usage

When Ruby runs out of slots, it executes GC to free up some memory. If GC can't free enough slots, Ruby increases the heap space as described earlier.

Ruby defines *enough slots* as either 20% of all allocated slots, or GC_HEAP_FREE_SLOTS (FREE_MIN in Ruby 2.0 and earlier), whichever is greater.

GC_HEAP_FREE_SLOTS/FREE_MIN is by default 4,096 slots. In practice, this value is too low, and gets used only once when Ruby increases the heap space for the first time. Because the initial number of slots as defined by GC_HEAP_INIT_SLOTS is 10,000, the *enough slots* rule is actually *free 40% of slots the first time and 20% afterward.*

Let's see how that works in irb. For simplicity, we'll use Ruby 1.9. Later versions behave the same, but they won't let us observe the effect easily because of the more complicated memory management.

```
$ rbenv shell 1.9.3-p551
$ irb
irb(main):001:0> GC.start
=> nil
irb(main):002:0> GC.stat
=> {:count=>7, :heap_used=>77, :heap_length=>77, :heap_increment=>0,
    :heap_live_num=>11939, :heap_free_num=>19365, :heap_final_num=>0}
```

During startup irb called GC six times and allocated 77 heaps. We called it one more time to ensure that heap_free_num will correctly estimate the number of free slots on the heap. This number is about 19,000.

If we allocate fewer objects than free slots we won't see GC:

```
irb(main):003:0> x = Array.new(15000) { Object.new }; nil
=> nil
irb(main):004:0> GC.stat.select { |k,v| [:count, :heap_used].include?(k) }
=> {:count=>7, :heap_used=>77}
```

As we've predicted, there was enough free space on the heap. Let's now unset the variable x to make all 15,000 objects in the array garbage, and allocate 15,000 objects again:

```
irb(main):005:0> x = nil
=> nil
irb(main):006:0> GC.stat.select { |k,v| [:count, :heap_used].include?(k) }
=> {:count=>7, :heap_used=>77}
irb(main):007:0> y = Array.new(15000) { Object.new }; nil
=> nil
irb(main):008:0> GC.stat.select { |k,v| [:count, :heap_used].include?(k) }
=> {:count=>8, :heap_used=>77}
```

This time when allocating our second array y, we didn't have enough free slots on the heap. So GC ran. However, it managed to reclaim enough free space. It freed all 15,000 objects from the array x. The heap space size at that time was 77 pages, approximately 31,000 slots on a 64-bit computer. So GC reclaimed about 50% of free space, more than the 20% threshold. This is why the heap space didn't grow and heap_used stayed the same.

Now if we allocate another 15,000 objects, GC will not be able to free enough space and the heap will grow:

```
irb(main):009:0> z = Array.new(15000) { Object.new }; nil
=> nil
irb(main):010:0> GC.stat.select { |k,v| [:count, :heap_used].include?(k) }
=> {:count=>9, :heap_used=>138}
```

This is exactly what happens. We see one more GC run, and the heap becomes 1.8 times bigger.

GC Triggered by Malloc Limit

Ruby objects can allocate extra memory outside of the Ruby heap space, and Ruby GC has little control over that memory. The only thing it can do to ensure Ruby objects don't use too much memory is to free as many unused objects as possible and hope that finalizing them reduces extra memory consumption.

That's why Ruby triggers GC by a memory limit. When we allocate more than the current limit, GC is forced regardless of how many free heap slots we have.

In Ruby 2.0 and earlier that limit is defined by a GC_MALLOC_LIMIT constant. Its default value is 8 million bytes, about 7.63 MB.

This means that every time we allocate additional 7.63 MB, GC will run. And this limit is too small.

What if our app is receiving 100 MB of data from the network in 10 MB batches? Get ready for at least 10 extra GC runs. Let's take a look:

```
$ rbenv shell 1.9.3-p551
$ irb

irb(main):001:0> data = "x"*1024*1024*10; nil
=> nil
irb(main):002:0> # store in array to keep data from garbage collection
irb(main):003:0* buffers = []
=> []
irb(main):004:0> GC.start
```

```
=> nil
irb(main):005:0> GC.stat[:count]
=> 9
irb(main):006:0> 10.times do |i|
irb(main):007:1*   buffers[i] = data.dup
irb(main):008:1>   # actually force Ruby to copy data in the memory
irb(main):009:1*   buffers[i][0] = 'a'
irb(main):010:1> end; nil
=> nil
irb(main):011:0> GC.stat[:count]
=> 21
```

For me Ruby ran GC 12 times, because every time I allocated more than the 7.63 MB limit, and some allocations actually exceeded the limit twice. You might see a slightly different number. But in any case it won't be far off from 10.

These days 7.63 MB is nothing. Your program will easily exceed this limit by doing trivial operations with data. So if you're using Ruby 2.0 or earlier, the malloc limit is the first parameter you'd want to tweak.

Admittedly, Ruby tries to adjust this limit at runtime. It takes the excess over the limit, adjusts it by a percentage of free space in the Ruby heap, and adds it to the current malloc limit.

For example, if our app uses 40% of the Ruby heap and allocates 10 MB, 2.37 MB over the limit, the malloc limit will be increased by 2.37 * 0.5 = 0.948 MB. And if it plans to continue allocating the 10 MB like our example did, the subsequent limit increases will be smaller and smaller. In any case, the limit will never exceed 10 MB with this algorithm.

So this malloc limit adaptation is not good enough for our example. In practice, I've rarely found it adequate, and tweaking it is a must.

Ruby 2.1 and later work slightly better. Just repeat the same irb session with the latest version. You'll see something like this:

```
$ rbenv shell 2.2.0
$ irb

irb(main):001:0> data = "x"*1024*1024*10; nil
=> nil
irb(main):002:0> # store in array to keep data from garbage collection
irb(main):003:0* buffers = []
=> []
irb(main):004:0> GC.start
=> nil
irb(main):005:0> GC.stat[:count]
=> 8
```

```
irb(main):006:0> 10.times do |i|
irb(main):007:1*   buffers[i] = data.dup
irb(main):008:1>   # actually force Ruby to copy data in the memory
irb(main):009:1*   buffers[i][0] = 'a'
irb(main):010:1> end; nil
=> nil
irb(main):011:0> GC.stat[:count]
=> 11
```

Having only 3 extra garbage collections is better than 11, isn't it? So let's see what the newest Ruby does better.

Ruby 2.1 introduced RGenGC—restricted generational GC. Ruby 2.2 adds RIncGC—incremental GC built on top of generational GC.

Here we'll talk about RGenGC and RIncGC only enough to understand their impact on performance. To learn more, read Aman Gupta's blog post[2] and watch Koichi Sasada's presentations.[3]

So how do RGenGC and RIncGC improve performance?

Generational GC divides all Ruby objects into two groups: a new generation and the old generation. An object becomes old when it survives at least one GC. Malloc limits for these generations are different: GC_MALLOC_LIMIT_MIN for the new generation and GC_OLDMALLOC_LIMIT_MIN for the old generation. Initial default values are the same, though: 16 MB.

The minimum 16 MB malloc limit is already a nice improvement over older Ruby. But even better is that it is allowed to grow up until GC_MALLOC_LIMIT_MAX (32 MB by default) for the new generation, and GC_OLDMALLOC_LIMIT_MAX (128 MB by default) for the old generation.

It is a good thing that the old generation's limit is larger because long-lived objects tend to be the ones to use more memory.

The malloc limit's growth factor no longer depends on the Ruby heap usage. Instead, it's fixed at GC_MALLOC_LIMIT_GROWTH_FACTOR (1.4 by default) for the new generation, and at GC_OLDMALLOC_LIMIT_GROWTH_FACTOR (1.2 by default) for the old generation. This way, Ruby is able to better adjust the GC settings when your program keeps allocating memory.

The growth factor for the new generation is larger. That allows it to quickly allocate memory without hitting GC. The growth factor for the old generation

---

2. http://tmm1.net/ruby21-rgengc/
3. https://vimeo.com/67807718
    https://www.youtube.com/watch?v=4UO60ocw52w

is smaller, but its malloc limit maximum is much larger. That allows the old generation to consume larger amounts of memory without the need for GC.

In practice, the new generations' malloc limit grows even faster because it applies not to the previous limit, but to the amount of memory your application has allocated since the last GC. That number is always bigger. So, for example, if our current limit is 16 MB and we're trying to allocate another 20 MB, then our next limit is 20 * 1.4 = 28 MB.

If our program doesn't allocate memory over the current limit anymore, Ruby gradually reduces it, decreasing by 0.98 times every time GC runs until the limit reaches GC_MALLOC_LIMIT_MIN or GC_OLDMALLOC_LIMIT_MIN.

Now we should be able to explain why our example triggers GC only three times.

We allocate 10 MB at a time, so only the second allocation will definitely exceed the 16 MB new generation malloc limit and trigger GC. At that time we'll be allocating 20 MB of memory since the last GC. So our next malloc limit will be 20 * 1.4 = 28 MB.

The fifth allocation will exceed the new limit, maxing it out at 32 MB because of the GC_MALLOC_LIMIT_MAX cap. Finally, the ninth allocation will be the last to exceed the limit and trigger GC. In total, this gives us the three GC runs that we saw when we ran our example.

GC#stat in Ruby 2.1 and later give us enough information to see for ourselves how well this theory corresponds to the practice.

Here are the malloc limit–related parameters:

malloc_limit (Ruby 2.1) or malloc_increase_bytes_limit (Ruby 2.2)
  Current malloc limit for the new generation.

malloc_increase (Ruby 2.1) or malloc_increase_bytes (Ruby 2.2)
  The amount of memory allocated by the new generation since the last GC.

oldmalloc_limit (Ruby 2.1) or oldmalloc_increase_bytes_limit (Ruby 2.2)
  Current malloc limit for the old generation.

oldmalloc_increase (Ruby 2.1) or oldmalloc_increase_bytes (Ruby 2.2)
  The amount of memory allocated by the new generation since the last GC.

So let's see at GC#stat the output in between allocations.

```
$ rbenv shell 2.2.0
$ irb
```

As before, we'll allocate the buffer and force GC to reset all malloc parameters for predictability:

```
irb(main):001:0> data = "x"*1024*1024*10; nil
=> nil
irb(main):002:0> buffers = []
=> []
irb(main):003:0> GC.start
=> nil
irb(main):004:0> [GC.stat[:count], GC.stat[:malloc_increase_bytes],
  GC.stat[:malloc_increase_bytes_limit]]
=> [8, 22816, 16777216]
```

Our theory predicted that we'll see the GC after the second allocation:

```
irb(main):005:0> buffers[0] = data.dup; buffers[0][0] = 'a'; nil
=> nil
irb(main):006:0> [GC.stat[:count], GC.stat[:malloc_increase_bytes],
  GC.stat[:malloc_increase_bytes_limit]]
=> [8, 10543000, 16777216]
irb(main):007:0> buffers[1] = data.dup; buffers[1][0] = 'a'; nil
=> nil
irb(main):008:0> [GC.stat[:count], GC.stat[:malloc_increase_bytes],
  GC.stat[:malloc_increase_bytes_limit]]
=> [9, 17032, 29464791]
```

Yes, that's exactly what we see. And the new malloc limit is 28 MB as expected. Let's continue with allocations:

```
irb(main):009:0> buffers[2] = data.dup; buffers[2][0] = 'a'; nil
=> nil
irb(main):010:0> [GC.stat[:count], GC.stat[:malloc_increase_bytes],
  GC.stat[:malloc_increase_bytes_limit]]
=> [9, 10537568, 29464791]
irb(main):011:0> buffers[3] = data.dup; buffers[3][0] = 'a'; nil
=> nil
irb(main):012:0> [GC.stat[:count], GC.stat[:malloc_increase_bytes],
  GC.stat[:malloc_increase_bytes_limit]]
=> [9, 21057392, 29464791]
irb(main):013:0> buffers[4] = data.dup; buffers[4][0] = 'a'; nil
=> nil
irb(main):014:0> [GC.stat[:count], GC.stat[:malloc_increase_bytes],
  GC.stat[:malloc_increase_bytes_limit]]
=> [10, 7616, 33554432]
```

Everything goes as expected so far: another GC after the fifth allocation, and the malloc limit is at its maximum.

```
irb(main):015:0> buffers[5] = data.dup; buffers[5][0] = 'a'; nil
=> nil
irb(main):016:0> [GC.stat[:count], GC.stat[:malloc_increase_bytes],
```

```
  GC.stat[:malloc_increase_bytes_limit]]
=> [10, 10488960, 33554432]
irb(main):017:0> buffers[6] = data.dup; buffers[6][0] = 'a'; nil
=> nil
irb(main):018:0> [GC.stat[:count], GC.stat[:malloc_increase_bytes],
  GC.stat[:malloc_increase_bytes_limit]]
=> [10, 21008104, 33554432]
irb(main):019:0> buffers[7] = data.dup; buffers[7][0] = 'a'; nil
=> nil
irb(main):020:0> [GC.stat[:count], GC.stat[:malloc_increase_bytes],
  GC.stat[:malloc_increase_bytes_limit]]
=> [10, 31528976, 33554432]
irb(main):021:0> buffers[8] = data.dup; buffers[8][0] = 'a'; nil
=> nil
irb(main):022:0> [GC.stat[:count], GC.stat[:malloc_increase_bytes],
  GC.stat[:malloc_increase_bytes_limit]]
=> [11, 16984, 33554432]
irb(main):023:0> buffers[9] = data.dup; buffers[9][0] = 'a'; nil
=> nil
irb(main):024:0> [GC.stat[:count], GC.stat[:malloc_increase_bytes],
  GC.stat[:malloc_increase_bytes_limit]]
=> [11, 10536160, 33554432]
```

As you see, our theory matches perfectly with the practice. The ninth allocation did the third GC run.

Now you know everything about what triggers GC. Armed with this knowledge, you can not only predict how often your own program will hit GC, but optimize it to reduce the number of collections.

Unsurprisingly, the best thing you can do to minimize GC is to upgrade to the most recent Ruby. It needs less GC, and that by itself is a significant optimization. But I'll tell you more. Each individual GC run itself is much faster in Ruby 2.1 and later. Let's see why.

Understand Why GC in Ruby 2.1 and 2.2 Is So Much Faster

In this book we repeatedly observed that new Ruby versions consistently perform better because the GC is faster. But why is it faster?

The first reason it's faster is that less GC is needed. We have just seen that with our memory allocation example. The second reason is that each individual GC run can take less time.

Ruby implements GC using a simple two-phase mark and sweep (M&S) algorithm. In the *mark* phase it finds all living objects on the Ruby heap and marks them as live. In the *sweep* phase it collects unmarked objects.

Naturally, GC can't allow you to allocate new objects while it marks. So your program pauses for the duration of GC.

Ruby 2.1 with RGenGC reduces the number of pauses, and Ruby with RIncGC optimizes the pause time.

RGenGC takes advantage of the fact that most objects die young. So most of the time GC needs to collect only the objects from the new generation. This is called *Minor GC*. *Major GC* happens when objects from both new and old generations are collected. Minor GC is very fast because it has fewer objects to mark and sweep, and most of the GC runs are minor—hence the optimization.

RIncGC performs the mark phase incrementally. It does not decrease the pause time, but rather distributes it. This way your program has a chance to finish its job in between incremental mark phases. Note that the overall GC time is not changed. So long-running code will see no difference between RGenGC and RIncGC. Refer to the Koichi Sasada's blog post[4] for a good visualization of this process.

Although we barely sketched Ruby GC internals, you should already understand why Ruby 2.1 and 2.2 perform so much better. If you are interested in GC architecture, there's no better description than Sasada's blog post or the recordings of his talks that I mentioned earlier.

While Ruby became faster out of the box in versions 2.1 and 2.2, it might still not perform optimally in your case. Depending on your object and memory allocation patterns, it might make sense to tweak Ruby GC for performance. Let's see how.

Tune Up GC Settings

We can change some of Ruby GC parameters with environment variables. Let's see what's available.

Ruby 2.1, 2.2, and Later

RUBY_GC_HEAP_INIT_SLOTS

Initial number of object slots on the Ruby heap. Default value is 10000.

You might want to change this number if you know that your application will allocate lots of objects right from the start.

---

4. https://engineering.heroku.com/blogs/2015-02-04-incremental-gc

But on the other hand, we saw that Ruby is quite good at growing the heap space. It usually grows faster than we need. So there's little need to change this parameter in practice.

RUBY_GC_HEAP_FREE_SLOTS

Minimum number of free slots that must be free after GC. If this condition is not met, Ruby might grow the heap space. Default value is 4096.

As we discussed in *GC Triggered by Heap Usage*, on page 162, the heap growth rule is more complicated. This value is used only once at runtime during the first heap growth after the initial one. So there's absolutely no need to change it.

RUBY_GC_HEAP_GROWTH_FACTOR

Heap growth factor. Default value is 1.8.

Ruby is already aggressive enough at heap growth, so you should not increase this number. Decreasing it also makes little sense. Heaps are allocated on demand in modern interpreters, so decreasing this number will not reduce the total memory consumption.

RUBY_GC_HEAP_GROWTH_MAX_SLOTS

Maximum number of slots Ruby can add to the heap space at a time. The default value is 0, meaning that there's no maximum.

If your application needs to allocate millions of objects during its lifetime, you might want to cap the heap growth increments by setting this value.

However, it will not help to reduce the GC time for such an application. Ruby is not the right tool to process lots of objects, and you should consider using other tools rather than trying to tweak Ruby.

RUBY_GC_HEAP_OLDOBJECT_LIMIT_FACTOR

This forces Ruby to do major GC when the number of old objects is more than RUBY_GC_HEAP_OLDOBJECT_LIMIT_FACTOR * <number of old objects after the last full GC>. The default value is 2.0.

In theory, you might want to increase this number if you expect that too many of your objects will become unused after getting into the old generation (surviving one GC in Ruby 2.1 and three in Ruby 2.2).

In practice, this is very rarely needed, and the default setting is good enough for most people.

RUBY_GC_MALLOC_LIMIT, RUBY_GC_MALLOC_LIMIT_MAX, RUBY_GC_MALLOC_LIMIT_GROWTH_FACTOR

> Minimum and maximum malloc limits for the new generation, and the limit's growth factor. The default values are 16 MB minimum, 32 MB maximum, 1.4 growth factor.
>
> These are the parameters you might want to change. If your application uses more memory than average, then increase the minimum and maximum values. If your application allocates memory in chunks, consider increasing the growth factor. There's little sense in decreasing these values.
>
> You might find advice on the Internet to set the minimum limit to 64 MB, or even 128 MB (that Twitter used at some point). But be careful. Larger limits lead to higher peak memory consumption.
>
> Increase the limits incrementally, adding, for example, 8 MB at a time, and measuring the outcome. Be even more careful changing the growth factor.
>
> I personally find that these days 50% of applications run just fine with the default settings, and another 50% benefit from a two times increase of minimum and maximum limits.

RUBY_GC_OLDMALLOC_LIMIT, RUBY_GC_OLDMALLOC_LIMIT_MAX, RUBY_GC_OLDMALLOC_LIMIT_GROWTH_FACTOR

> Minimum and maximum malloc limits for the old generation, and the limit's growth factor. The default values are 16 MB minimum, 128 MB maximum, 1.2 growth factor.
>
> These are also candidates for tweaking. It's a good idea to change them together with the limits for new generation, and in the same manner.

Ruby 2.0, 1.9, and Earlier

Older Ruby versions require recompilation to change all their settings except these three:

RUBY_HEAP_MIN_SLOTS

> Same as `RUBY_GC_HEAP_INIT_SLOTS` in newer Ruby.

RUBY_FREE_MIN

> Same as `RUBY_GC_HEAP_FREE_SLOTS` in newer Ruby.

RUBY_GC_MALLOC_LIMIT

> One malloc limit for non-generational GC. The default value is 8,000,000 bytes.

You absolutely must change this value. 8 MB limit is too small, and will lead to more GC runs than necessary. Increase it to at least 16 MB. Then, continue adding 8 MB and testing the outcomes until you find your sweet spot.

There's no way to change GC parameters without recompilation in Ruby 1.8. If you still use that version, consider switching to the more configurable Ruby Enterprise Edition.[5] Just like Ruby 1.9 and 2.0, Ruby 1.8 needs a larger malloc limit for better performance.

Let's quickly review. The only parameter that makes a difference in performance is the malloc limit. You must change it for older Ruby versions, and consider a slight increase for newer versions. Other parameters have either good default values for most cases, or make no sense to change.

Takeaways

Ruby GC is not a black box. Once you understand how it works, you can either change your code to put less strain on it, or you can tune GC up for better performance. Here's what you need to keep in mind:

- Ruby allocates objects on a dedicated heap space, which it manages itself.

- Each object has the fixed amount of storage (40 bytes on 64-bit computers). If the object needs more memory, it allocates that on the operating system heap.

- Ruby runs GC when it decides that it allocated too many objects or its objects allocated too much memory. Correspondingly, there are two criteria for this decision. First, Ruby heap space doesn't have enough free slots. Second, the current memory allocation (malloc) limit has been exceeded.

- You can tweak most GC parameters for optimal performance. In practice, however, it makes sense to change only memory allocation limits. If you use Ruby 2.0 or earlier, you must increase RUBY_GC_MALLOC_LIMIT at least twice. If you use Ruby 2.1 and later, you may not need to change anything. In any case, make sure you measure the performance after the change.

---

5. http://www.rubyenterpriseedition.com

Onward!

Performance optimization is a never-ending battle. New code will slow down the old code. And even the old code you can make faster and faster if you spend enough time on it.

I've found that the same applies to this book. I could always add more techniques and best practices. There's always one more optimization tool that I didn't cover. That's why I created a wiki page[6] with additional resources other readers and I found useful for optimization. You're welcome to use and contribute to it.

Now it's time for you to optimize your code.

First, find and fix all performance blunders. We talked about many of them in the first three chapters, so now you'll spot them just by looking at the code.

Then, see what your logging and monitoring tools report as slow. Isolate the underperforming parts, and profile them. Understand what makes them slow, optimize, measure. Rinse and repeat as necessary. Write a test that will ensure your optimization will not vanish as you change the code.

Finally, step back and rethink how your code runs. You'll be surprised how fine-tuning your application's environment makes things faster.

And remember, always measure the effect of any change you make. Not only will you know whether the optimization worked, but you'll have something to be proud of.

Wouldn't it be so cool to report 74 times speedup in the commit log? Go ahead and optimize. I'm sure you'll do that, and even better!

---

6. https://github.com/ruby-performance-book/resources/wiki

Index

Facets of Ruby

Definitive Ruby information for all developers.

Programming Ruby 1.9 & 2.0 (4th edition)

Ruby is the fastest growing and most exciting dynamic language out there. If you need to get working programs delivered fast, you should add Ruby to your toolbox.

This book is the only complete reference for both Ruby 1.9 and Ruby 2.0, the very latest version of Ruby.

Dave Thomas, with Chad Fowler and Andy Hunt
(888 pages) ISBN: 9781937785499. $50
https://pragprog.com/book/ruby4

Metaprogramming Ruby 2

Write powerful Ruby code that is easy to maintain and change. With metaprogramming, you can produce elegant, clean, and beautiful programs. Once the domain of expert Rubyists, metaprogramming is now accessible to programmers of all levels. This thoroughly revised and updated second edition of the bestselling *Metaprogramming Ruby* explains metaprogramming in a down-to-earth style and arms you with a practical toolbox that will help you write your best Ruby code ever.

Paolo Perrotta
(278 pages) ISBN: 9781941222126. $38
https://pragprog.com/book/ppmetr2

Applying Ruby in the Real World

Use the power of Ruby to get the job done.

Agile Web Development with Rails 4

Rails just keeps on changing. Both Rails 3 and 4, as well as Ruby 1.9 and 2.0, bring hundreds of improvements, including new APIs and substantial performance enhancements. The fourth edition of this award-winning classic has been reorganized and refocused so it's more useful than ever before for developers new to Ruby and Rails.

Rails 4 introduces a number of user-facing changes, and the book has been updated to match all the latest changes and new best practices in Rails. This includes full support for Ruby 2.0, controller concerns, Russian Doll caching, strong parameters, Turbolinks, new test and bin directory layouts, and much more.

Sam Ruby
(456 pages) ISBN: 9781937785567. $43.95
https://pragprog.com/book/rails4

Build Awesome Command-Line Applications in Ruby 2

Speak directly to your system. With its simple commands, flags, and parameters, a well-formed command-line application is the quickest way to automate a backup, a build, or a deployment and simplify your life. With this book, you'll learn specific ways to write command-line applications that are easy to use, deploy, and maintain, using a set of clear best practices and the Ruby programming language. This book is designed to make *any* programmer or system administrator more productive in their job. This is updated for Ruby 2.

David Copeland
(224 pages) ISBN: 9781937785758. $30
https://pragprog.com/book/dccar2

The Pragmatic Bookshelf

The Pragmatic Bookshelf features books written by developers for developers. The titles continue the well-known Pragmatic Programmer style and continue to garner awards and rave reviews. As development gets more and more difficult, the Pragmatic Programmers will be there with more titles and products to help you stay on top of your game.

Visit Us Online

This Book's Home Page
https://pragprog.com/book/adrpo
Source code from this book, errata, and other resources. Come give us feedback, too!

Register for Updates
https://pragprog.com/updates
Be notified when updates and new books become available.

Join the Community
https://pragprog.com/community
Read our weblogs, join our online discussions, participate in our mailing list, interact with our wiki, and benefit from the experience of other Pragmatic Programmers.

New and Noteworthy
https://pragprog.com/news
Check out the latest pragmatic developments, new titles and other offerings.

Save on the eBook

Save on the eBook versions of this title. Owning the paper version of this book entitles you to purchase the electronic versions at a terrific discount.

PDFs are great for carrying around on your laptop—they are hyperlinked, have color, and are fully searchable. Most titles are also available for the iPhone and iPod touch, Amazon Kindle, and other popular e-book readers.

Buy now at *https://pragprog.com/coupon*

Contact Us

Online Orders: *https://pragprog.com/catalog*
Customer Service: *support@pragprog.com*
International Rights: *translations@pragprog.com*
Academic Use: *academic@pragprog.com*
Write for Us: *http://write-for-us.pragprog.com*
Or Call: +1 800-699-7764

Ingram Content Group UK Ltd.
Milton Keynes UK
UKHW032023140723
425157UK00012B/310